This Sporting Life
CRICKET

Rob Steen

This Sporting Life
CRICKET

Inside tales from the men who made
the game what it is today

DAVID & CHARLES

A DAVID & CHARLES BOOK

First published in the UK in 1999

Copyright © Rob Steen 1999

A catalogue record for this book is available from the British Library.

ISBN 0 7153 0851 3

Printed in Great Britain by Redwood Books Ltd, Trowbridge, Wilts
for David & Charles
Brunel House   Newton Abbot   Devon

Contents

To Evie: may your edges always fall safely

The Foreword

WHEN JOHN ARLOTT, the greatest of all cricket commentators, held sway on the radio, people would listen to him specially, sometimes even switching off when his colleagues took over. 'You see, he doesn't talk about the cricket,' they would explain.

Well, of course, he talked about the cricket. But he didn't *just* talk about the cricket. He made connections. He drew analogies. He tied the game in to real life. In the hands of less skilful operators, this sort of thing can turn into mere irrelevant chatter. But Arlott, the master, understood instinctively where the line should be: how much the cricket mattered; how much it didn't matter.

Everyone who loves cricket does so in the context of the rest of their lives. Football lasts 90 minutes and usually takes place in the evening or weekends. Cricket goes on when most people are at work. If there's a Test match taking place, they may be able to discover the score only furtively: the hidden earphone; the quick visit to the loo; the Internet score tucked into the corner of their computer screen.

Even the professionals – the writers, the players, the umpires – have to fit the game in to the other details of their existence. Even Dickie Bird, the most famous and extreme of cricketing obsessives, doesn't actually eat and sleep cricket. (Oh, all right, maybe Dickie's an exception). But the nature and beauty of cricket is that it does fit in. There is always analogy. There is always context. One of Rob Steen's great skills as a writer is that he understands that.

Rob and I have a secret shared vice. When finances and our families permit, we try to sneak off to America in the summer and watch a few days' baseball together. Other cricket writers clearly think we're barmy. (And heaven knows what the Americans make of us if they ever overhear an argument about the structure of the County Championship over the hot dogs and pretzels during quiet moments at Shea Stadium or Wrigley Field.) But cricket and baseball are long-lost brothers, and the tiny handful of people in the world (the Chappell brothers being perhaps the most distinguished) who enjoy both games find their understanding of both enriched because they can make connections.

I think Rob has enough sense not to start blathering about baseball to the wrong people in cricket. But it helps his perspective, and enhances his ability to talk to cricket people, and persuade them to make all kinds of connections between cricket and the other corners of their own lives. 'He doesn't just write about the cricket,' you might say. That makes him a far more interesting writer than someone who only knows about off and leg stumps.

These days, I edit *Wisden Cricketers' Almanack*, traditionally the ultimate book for cricket fanatics. But one of the things I've tried to impress on all our writers is the importance of what you might call Arlottian irrelevance. *Wisdens* from the nineteenth century are still read enthusiastically now, and we proceed in the hope and belief that the volumes from the end of the twentieth and the start of the twenty-first centuries will be read just as enthusiastically at the start of the twenty-second.

The least interesting bits of the old books are the pure cricketing details. Who cares whether some Victorian was caught at mid-on or mid-off? It's the context of the game that's fascinating, the social history, the amount we learn about the way life was lived at the time: how different these people were from us – and how similar.

This volume, I think, will have the same sort of enduring appeal. Lord Sheppard, Brian Close, Alf Gover and the other characters are human beings. It is their humanity, and the way their cricketing lives are part of that, which is so compelling. And it is the humanity of cricket as a whole, more than anything else, which explains why so many apparently intelligent men and women spend so much of their time playing it, watching it and nattering about it.

MATTHEW ENGEL
Newton St Margarets, Herefordshire, April 1999

The Prologue

'GOD GAVE US baseball to make up for the Industrial Revolution.' Goldie Hawn's lover proffered that snappy little homily in the movie *Criss Cross*. Swap the invention of the twenty-four-hour day for the Industrial Revolution and much the same could be said of cricket, another sport ritually held up as a mirror of all the things that make a nation preen. The Luddites of the greensward, nonetheless, are still up in arms.

To British cricket lovers of a certain age (and this really does tend to be a generational thing), the summer of 1998 was a perplexing one. Make that an unnerving one. Granted, the national team contrived to win a five-Test series for the first time in twelve seemingly endless years – and after coming from behind at that. There was also a richly-merited county championship title for dear old Leicestershire, a team in the truest meaning of the word. A Sri Lankan spinner, furthermore, spellbound partisan and neutral alike at The Oval with one of the most dazzling feats the five-day game has ever witnessed. Swirling around, however, were the gusts of change, not all greeted with undiluted enthusiasm.

After more than a century, the first-class counties approved a two-tiered championship, having gone halfway there the previous summer by voting in a similar structure for the planned National League. After twenty-seven seasons, the Benson and Hedges Cup died an unlamented death; after thirty seasons, the Sunday League, bane of purists and techniques, died an unlamented death. A profusion of floodlit games were staged up and down the land, improving options for those in employment and/or at school – albeit some twenty years after the Australians had got the message. For the first time, a triangular international one-day tourney was held on these shores – again some two decades after the Aussies thought of it. The BBC introduced a nifty little device enabling viewers to zoom in on the ball as never before, undermining umpires as never before. The MCC finally consented to invite the fillies to join its seventeen-year waiting list for membership. 'Gosh,' smirked the ageing platinum blonde newscaster on CNN, 'don't you think they're rushing things here?'

Amid all this uproar and upheaval, I spoke to a diverse group of men representing The Way We Were (And Shall Never Be Again). The age of three-day championship matches on uncovered pitches, of batsmen without helmets and bowlers without a prayer, of packed houses on Saturdays and feet up on Sundays. When the England team was more frequently a source of pride than embarrassment (all right, it is not utterly inconceivable that that might yet recur ...)

The categories were straightforward enough: as many compartments filled as possible. I settled on ten: bowler, batsman, captain, coach, umpire, scorer, administrator, writer, commentator and weekend devotee. I had to draw the line somewhere, so profuse apologies in advance to any women/wicketkeepers/groundsmen/attendants/tea persons I may thus have offended. I should also like to take this opportunity to convey my regrets to John Shepherd, that splendid Bajan all-rounder who graced Canterbury and Bristol during the Sixties and Seventies: we never quite managed that dinner, did we? Ah well. Still, two crook-wielders on one contents page is rather pushing it.

Although budgetary restrictions prevented the sort of globetrotting a book of this nature would ideally necessitate, I have striven not to make it too parochial. The titans of the Caribbean feature prominently, likewise those of Australia and New Zealand, India and Pakistan, South Africa and North England. And who better to speak for the international game than my chosen administrator, Ali Bacher, chairman of the International Cricket Council's development committee?

More, though, than simply filling boxes, I made my choices in a way that would at least make it possible to sketch out cricket's evolution over the last – well, however many years it was possible to go back. As a starting-point, who better than Alf Gover, the oldest surviving Test player? In consequence, the ensuing chapters cover the development of the game since the Great War, from Gover all the way to Bacher, David Foot, John Harris and Byron Denning, all still heavily involved in 1998. Through their eyes we alight on the issues, incidents and personalities responsible for shaping the game: from bodyline and limited-overs to D'Oliveira and unlimited TV replays; from scorecards starring Bennett D.B. to scorecards starring D.B. Bennett; from back-foot no-balls to bouncer restrictions; from umpires in white to umpires in powder blue; from scorebook to PC; from Hobbs to Ntini via Bradman and Sobers, Zaheer and Botham. From Peter West live at the Kennington Oval to Mark Nicholas live at the Kensington Oval. From Brian Close, the gutsiest man ever to play the game, to Geoffrey Gowland, the noisiest. From David Sheppard to The Rt Rev Lord Sheppard. From alleged Utopia to purported purgatory.

Through it all, I trust, the humanity shines brightest. Men behaving boldly, men behaving badly, men behaving madly. Each of them playing up and playing the game. May their edges always fall safely.

ROB STEEN
Alexandra Palace, April 1999

Chapter 1:
The Bowler's Tale:

'Batsmen are like eggs in summer – eighteen a shilling – but bowlers, real ones, are as rare as a Lord's lunch to a professional cricketer when winter has set in.'

'Dicky' Barlow, quoted by Fred Root, *A Cricket Pro's Lot* (1937)

The fifteenth of June 1998. England's opening match of the World Cup is barely a couple of hours away and the team's so-called 'supporters' are doing their level best to lay waste to downtown Marseilles, upholding the nation's increasingly proud traditions for poor guestmanship; London, meanwhile, is in the grip of a rather different reign of terror – a Tube strike. Alf Gover may have turned ninety the best part of four months ago but his sideboard is still swamped with cards. From Karachi and Kalgoorlie, Barbados and Bombay, Birmingham and Bermondsey. 'I'm only twenty-two-and-a-bit y'know,' he chirps, pointing out that he was born in a leap year. For sheer vim and vigour, he could pass for it, too.

The first thing you notice is how tall and straight-backed he is. Not a millimetre shorter, so far as the naked eye can ascertain, than when he was in his six-foot-three-plus pomp. Imagine a moose standing on its hind legs and you'll get a rough idea. The next thing you notice are those huge, tapering, spidery fingers. Small wonder he was one of the elite band of fast bowlers ever to take 200 wickets in a season, not only becoming the first to do so this century (in 1936) but doing it again the following summer. Under that sort of manual pressure, what choice did the ball have *but* to obey?

The next thing you notice is that he is far more eager to talk about others, a highly unusual, not to say refreshing trait for a sporting hero. Colleagues and captains, mentors and pupils, opponents and pals. Twice during our two-hour conversation I asked him for recollections of his Test career. Twice he responded with little more than sketches. Given that there weren't that many to rewind (four matches to be precise), and that his memory for less personal details was largely spot-on, I had confidently expected chapter and verse, complete with litany of complaints. Not a bit of it. He even managed to reflect on his final appearance, at his beloved Kennington Oval in 1946, without referring to the fact that during its course he was directly responsible for one of the game's most indelible

'So I said to Larwood...' Alf Gover, at home in Keith Miller's old Putney flat, 1998. Inset: Those never-ending, unwithered fingers – what choice did the ball have but to obey? (*Graham Goldwater*)

Signature tune... Alf obliges
some young admirers
during a benefit game
(*Alf Gover Collection*)

The other woman... Alf (*far right*),
the first professional cricketer to be
elected president of the Golf
Society; second from left is Colin
Cowdrey (*Alf Gover Collection*)

Below: Diamond geezers... rain
wrecked Alf's final Test, against India
at his beloved Kennington Oval in
1946, leaving him to form an
illustrious card school (*from left*):
Sandy Tait (trainer), Len Hutton, Joe
Hardstaff, Cyril Washbrook, Alf and
Denis Compton. At Alf's urging,
Compton would run out one of the
Indians with a shot more befitting
Wembley (*Hulton Getty*)

moments, urging Denis Compton (ex-Arsenal) to run out that prolific Indian opener Vijay Merchant with his trusty left foot.

Then again, Alf Gover is renowned as much by association as for his own accomplishments. Not that those can be sniffed at. Besides harvesting 1555 first-class wickets at 23.63 apiece, most of them on those heartbreaking batsmen-friendly Oval pitches of the Twenties and Thirties, and covering the game over the ensuing decades as an astute Fleet Street scribe, he ran the world's most famous cricket school for more than forty years, turning a handsome profit in addition to aiding the careers of many of the game's most luminous practitioners. More significantly, his life is a thread connecting sepia-hued past to techni-colour present.

Yet the most compelling thing about Alfred Richard Gover MBE (the gong was bestowed in the 1998 New Year's Honours) is not that the framed photo gallery on his hall wall features a snapshot of that unforgettable day he shared a century stand with his beloved Jack Hobbs. Nor that he postponed his wed-ding to play in the annual charity match at Wimbledon organised by 'The Master'. Nor that when the so-called Master's Club first convened in 1954 – lunches were henceforth held before every Lord's and Oval Test and on Hobbs' birthday – he was responsible for instituting the traditional toast: 'To The Master'.

Nor that he once clean-bowled Herbert Sutcliffe and Maurice 'The Unbowlable' Leyland on the same day, nor that Harold Larwood once struck him amidships – and apologised. Nor that he dared to defy Douglas Jardine. Nor that he had the similarly barefaced gall to apprise Don Bradman of the fact that he didn't mind bowling to him in the least. Nor that he inspired two Ashes tri-umphs: it was he who remodelled Jim Laker's approach to the stumps, paving the way for that inimitable easeful jog; it was he who advised Len Hutton to tell Frank Tyson to trim his run ('Len told him I was the one who knew and he'd better do it').

Nor that he also coached Gary Sobers, Hanif Mohammed, Viv Richards and Ian Botham (not forgetting John Major). Nor that he originally bought the cricket school from those Surrey and England lions of the Roaring Twenties, Herbert Strudwick and Andy Sandham. Nor that, at the time of our meeting, he was residing in the selfsame apartment once rented by Australia's own Lancelot-cum-Biggles, Keith Miller. Nor that his own debut for England, at Old Trafford in 1936, yielded the most runs ever amassed in a single day of a Test. Nor even that, at a wintry Oval a couple of months previously, he and the rest of the Surrey lads had taken a tea break on the field – complete with pot and strainer.

No, the most compelling thing about Alfred Richard Gover MBE is his staunch refusal to ridicule all things modern. Indeed, as one of the original advocates of the limited-overs format as a necessary adjunct to a game fast falling into a commercial coma, he actually enthuses about it. Which, for an Englishman born in the first half of the twentieth century, may well make him unique. Which is why I chose him to carry the torch.

EVEN AS A babe in arms Alf could scarcely avoid cricket. His Epsom birthplace overlooked the local club. Unfortunately, in the aftermath of the Great War, batting and bowling was not especially high on the list of priorities at St Mary's, Merton. For one thing, this south London scholastic emporium had no sports ground to call its own. Not that that daunted Alf and his pals. Espying potential in a neighbouring field, they pooled their resources and pocket money. One lad borrowed the family lawnmower. Another persuaded his father, a builder, to lend them his roller. Another purloined a pair of shears, the upshot an adequate pitch and a passable outfield. For stumps read branches. A local junk shop furnished a couple of bats and a rubber composite ball. 'The ball had to last the whole season,' stresses Alf. 'If somebody hit it into the trees there was no question of a lost ball: the game had to stop until we found it.' Oversized pads, courtesy of another father, were pared down by dutiful mothers. It was Alf's mother, indeed, who would encourage him most.

A rough and ready initiation to be sure, but invaluable for all that. 'I always wanted to bowl fast,' reflects Alf. 'I always opened the bowling – I was the fastest around, tearing in, holding the ball like an apple, aiming straight at the stumps. I just wanted to bowl fast. I suppose it must have had something to do with the physical exhilaration. My hero was Bill Hitch. I saw him at The Oval as a small boy. Saved up all my pocket money to go. Small bloke, a skidder. He had a very distinctive action – seven paces, hop, seven paces, hop, seven paces, hop. I decided I wanted to be Bill Hitch. "I'm Bill Hitch," I'd say to my mates when we played in that field. I met him some years later when he'd gone to Glamorgan as coach. I told him he'd been my hero. "Well," he said, "that's very nice. I've been watching your bowling. You've got a good action." I told him I'd tried to copy him but obviously without much luck. Lovely man.

'I had a long run for a while then I cut it back to seventeen paces. Jack Lodge, my old cricket master at school, wrote to me once saying he'd like to come and see me play, so I left two complimentary tickets at the gate for him. He came in at the Vauxhall End when I was bowling, he told me afterwards. "I knew it was you," he said. "Your action hasn't changed a bit."'

Alf was seventeen and the General Strike beckoning when, after a few outings for the local YMCA upon leaving St Mary's, he grasped the bull by the proverbials. Obtaining the address of the secretary of the West Wimbledon club, he knocked on his door and blithely informed him that he could bowl fairly nippily and bat a bit, too. 'What makes you think you're good enough for us?' harrumphed the secretary. 'Don't you worry about that,' retorted Alf. The next step was rather more problematic.

'I was working for a building firm, which I continued to do in the winters when I became a professional. I'd almost qualified as a quantity surveyor; my dad was a chartered surveyor. One day a chap at the office, who happened to be an Essex member, asked me what I was going to be doing in my two-week summer holiday. "Playing cricket," I told him, only there wasn't any in my neck of the woods. "Well," he said, "I know Essex Club and Ground are short of players and they've got a game coming up." So he recommended me, and I went along to Chelmsford. I never mentioned that I was only seeking a few holiday games. The Essex secretary told me to report to the big man out in the nets – Charlie McGahey, lovely fella. So I did. "What's your name?" he asked. "Gover," I replied. "You're supposed to be quick, aren't you?" he said. "Well, bowl at this fella." Well, I ended up hitting this fella once or twice in a fiery fifteen-minute spell, and when I asked Charlie who it was, he told me it was [former England captain] Johnny Douglas.

'"Oh my God," I thought. "I'll see you in my dressing-room, boy," said Johnny sternly. He always used to talk like that, a bit sergeant-majorish. "Right," I thought, I'm for it now. He's going to tell me off. So I went to his room. "Hmm, got a bit of pace on you, boy," he said. "Thank you sir," I replied. "What club do you play for?" he asked, thinking I was going to say Chingford or one of those other Essex clubs. "Well," I said, "West Wimbledon, sir." So he turned to Charlie and said "Where the hell's that, Charlie? Wimbledon? Wimbledon? That's where they play tennis." Then he asked me where I was born. "Epsom, overlooking the cricket club," I said. "Ah, pfah," he said to Charlie. "We find a fast bowler and he's not even eligible. Get him qualified, Charlie."

'To get a residential qualification they booked a room for me in Leyton. I played for the Club and Ground side and the second XI. One day, having noticed that there were no minor games the following Saturday, I asked the secretary whether I could go and be twelfth man for the firsts at The Oval. "Cor," I thought, if I can just get into the same dressing-room as my heroes – Hobbs, Sandham, Hitch, Fender. The Surrey scorer then was Herbert Strudwick and when I went down there he introduced himself. He knew I was a fast bowler and, since Essex were only fielding one, he wondered why I wasn't playing. "You should be with us, not them," he said. So he arranged for me to be given the once-over by the Surrey coach, "Razor" Smith. I got myself away from Essex and came to The Oval in '28.'

Even though he would soon be earning as much as a bank manager – while still going back to surveying in the winter – the decision to turn pro was not an entirely popular one. 'Mum encouraged me but Dad didn't approve of professional sportsmen, although he came round when I made it. My wife was always supportive but she never took that much interest. Before we were married, Ada, Jack Hobbs' wife, met her round the back of the Oval pavilion one day and told her: "If you're going to marry that man you'd better watch him play." So she did, and she watched when she could, before we had children. Her father ran his own team but she didn't know anything about the game really. We never discussed it much. It was my job. "Got five wickets today, dear," I'd say. "Oh, very nice," she'd reply – and that was that. My son *hated* it when I got wickets. When he came to The Oval he wanted to see runs.'

GRANTED, FRANK KELLOGG and Aristide Briand may have drawn up the Pact for the Renunciation of War, but in most other respects 1928 was a pretty good year for mavericks and iconoclasts. Amelia Earhart flew the Atlantic. Berlin saw the public debut of Bertolt Brecht and Kurt Weill's *Threepenny Opera*; Paris the first performance of Maurice Ravel's *Bolero*; London the premiere of Edgar Wallace's *The Terror*, the world's first all-talking, all-screaming movie. Compton Mackenzie's *Extraordinary Women* was published, as was Evelyn Waugh's *Decline and Fall*. Stanley Kubrick, Karlheinz Stockhausen and Andy Warhol all shuffled on to this mortal coil. During the first official West Indies tour of England, Learie Constantine, one of the few black members of the party, son of a plantation foreman in Trinidad, grandson of a slave and a future member of the House of Lords, electrified the other Lord's: 86 in half an hour to lead a first-innings recovery against Middlesex, followed by seven for 57 and a whirlwind match-winning hundred. Alf, meanwhile, was exposed to that titan of tactics and tactlessness, Percy George Herbert Fender – wine merchant, all-rounder, scorer of the fastest *bona fide* century in first-class history, inventor of the reverse sweep and the greatest captain England never had.

One reason proffered for Fender being overlooked as his country's leader was his militant tendency. He had the effrontery, after all, to lead amateurs and professionals on to the field through the same gate. He even proposed, albeit fruitlessly, that they share the same dressing-room. Worse, he took on Lord Harris, arguably the single most influential figure English cricket has ever known, failing to tug forelock with sufficient conviction. Another theory related to his alleged Jewishness (his nose was large and unmistakably cheeky). 'Well, he was cut like a Jew, from what I saw in the showers,' chuckles Alf. He, for one, believes anti-Semitism had sod all to do with it.

'Percy George was an awkward chap, the type who, if he asked you to have dinner with him while we were playing away and staying in a hotel, within half an hour he'd have a row. Extraordinary, quite contrary, not scared of ruffling feathers, but very kind, the finest cricket brain I ever came across and the best captain I ever played under. Everything I have done I owe to Percy George. And I assure you I'm not saying that because he was the only decent slip fielder I ever had at Surrey.'

Alf was in his customary position of forward short leg at Trent Bridge when Fender pulled off one of his most brazen coups. He had warned Alf that he would tug his collar when he was about to deliver a seductive legside full-toss to Arthur Carr, the Nottinghamshire captain and progenitor of Bodyline, whereupon Alf was supposed to fling himself to the turf. 'After an over or two Percy George tugged at his collar,' he would tell Fender's estimable biographer, Dick Streeton. 'I ducked as Carr swung wildly. It was still high in the air as Fender called out "Carr, caught Gregory, bowled Fender", and so it was. Fender and Carr stood together in the middle of the pitch and watched Gregory take the catch on the midwicket boundary. "You so-and-so," Carr said. It amused us because we knew Fender was staying at Carr's house.'

So to the key question. Who was the superior leader of men: Jardine or Fender? No contest, apparently. 'Jardine was an amateur with a professional approach,' wrote Alf in his affectionate yet punchy autobiography, *The Long Run*, published when he was a spry eighty-three – and without the aid of a ghost. 'He hated Australians,' he says now, 'because they got at him over his Harlequin cap, so he wore it just to annoy them more.'

'He never gave a thing away,' he told Streeton, 'but with Percy George, for instance, it was always understood that we conceded a single if a new batsman came in to the non-striker's end. Nothing would be said, but everyone surreptitiously went back a few yards. That was the way the bowler could get at the new man before he got used to the light. It wasn't too important, I suppose, but Fender was the only captain I knew who regularly rang the Air Ministry Roof for the weather forecasts. That was the place to go before the days of TV weather centres; they were often wrong, but Percy George would make allowances for that too.'

Fender inculcated the young Alf with much of his own philosophy of self-affirmation. '"My side does not need your batting, Gover," he told me. "I want you to think bowling, day and night. Always think you are better than any batsman because you are." If things were going badly he'd say: "Can you manage one more over?" And perhaps you'd get a wicket and then you'd want to stay on. He would go through the motions of saying "I only asked you for one" and you'd end up pleading to carry on. Then you felt you *had* to deliver the goods. All along, of course, that was the frame of mind he wanted to get you into. After he retired we became good friends. I used to go down to Sussex to see him. His business went off and he went down to live with his mother by the sea. He was obviously a bit pushed. We had a bottle of wine at lunch and he insisted, "I mustn't have too much". I still called him Skip, so he told me to call him George. "Oh no," I said, "I can't do that."'

BEGINNING AS IT did the year before the ball shrank (to its present minimum circumference of eight and 13/16 ins), Alf's playing career spanned two generations of Hardstaffs, two coalition governments, a world war, the inception of the NHS, Cardiff City and Charlton Athletic winning the FA Cup, even a Brit winning the men's singles at Wimbledon. And no end of upheavals on the greensward.

Trains gave way to cars as the preferred mode of transport between fixtures. 'Jack Hobbs, who earned the same per summer as me, £600, the top whack, was the first player to have one, in the days when they cost a coupla hundred quid, and I used to go with him quite a lot; prior to that the trainer used to collect all our bags at Greenwich and put them on the train – it was six and a half hours to Scarborough.'

The county championship of 1936, to pluck one at random, might best be described as higgledy-piggledy: teams played anything between twenty-four and thirty-two three-day fixtures on uncovered pitches, the title was decided on proportions and percentages, and a match drawn with the scores level was worth seven and a half points per protagonist; by 1945, a one-day competition was being proposed (all right, so it took another eighteen years to see the light of day). Within a couple of years of Alf's retirement those commonplace five-figure gates, boosted by high unemployment and cut-price admission in the Thirties and postwar euphoria in the Forties, began to dwindle towards the present gaggle. Never again would county cricket mean so much to so many.

Ask a fast bowler to characterise the game he plays and his response can be relied upon to comprise the words 'a', 'batsman's' and 'game', and never more so than in the Thirties. The Oval was no exception. 'All that changed with the appointment of "Bosser" Martin as groundsman after the war,' asserts Alf. 'We called him "Bosser" because that's what he was: the boss. He was there at six every morning. Always had his sleep after lunch. Knocked the runs out of the square.' All of which was excellent news for the likes of Bedser, Laker, Lock and Loader, albeit a bit late in the day for Alf.

That said, measures were taken to tilt the odds. In 1931, the stumps, at the last count twenty-seven inches by eight, gained an inch in height, giving Alf and his beleaguered breed some long-overdue if modest encouragement. In 1937, better yet, it became possible to glean an lbw verdict from a delivery pitched outside off stump. In 1947 came further succour with the introduction of the back-foot no-ball rule, whereby some part of the rear foot had to be behind the popping crease; inevitably, this bred a generation of pacemen who, by dragging their rear boot to the brink of the line, succeeded in discharging their arrows from a couple of yards nearer. Alf holds his hands up: 'I dragged. So did Larwood, a hell of a lot. And loads of others. I had trouble adjusting, no-balling a lot through over-striding. But I still think they were wrong to discard it. It gives the umpire an extra split-second more time to concentrate on what happens at the other end.'

When Alf joined Surrey he would not have looked out of place on a plate of sushi. 'I was very raw. I just held the ball alongside the seam and let it go as fast as I could. While Percy George advised me on tactics, all the coaching as regards my action came from Struddy [Strudwick]. "Keep your left arm up," he told me, "and look at the spot where you want to pitch it." Then, after three years, Percy George asked me into his dressing-room to meet Frank Foster, one of the game's legends, notably for having helped S.F. Barnes beat the Aussies in 1910–11. Frank was supposed to teach me how to bowl swing. We talked for well over an hour, standing in front of the big mirror in the dressing-room, going through everything: the motions of the action, how to grip the ball, the importance of having the hand behind the ball at the moment of release, position of the shoulders at the crease, co-ordination of the arms for delivery, as well as the mental side. "Remember," he said, "to be able to bowl fast is a gift and an art." Controlling length and direction, the amount of swing by using the crease, the timing of release – I hadn't thought of it in that way before, but it *is* an art.'

Upon his arrival at The Oval Alf was paid a 'small' weekly salary from January to December plus a match fee whenever he was selected for the first XI. The club, furthermore, guaranteed his earnings would be at least £400; throw in appearance money and the sum could come to £500 or more. He also had the sense to follow his colleagues' lead, taking out insurance to cover matches missed through injury or mishap. Medical facilities, needless to add, were somewhat primitive. After bursting out of the blocks with a spate of wickets in 1936, he was stricken with lumbago: 'Sandy Tait, the trainer, gave me some heat treatment, massaged me for a while, did some physiotherapy, then stuck a Belladonna plaster over my lower back, strapped it up with Elastoplast and told the skipper I'd be OK to bowl so long as I didn't make any sudden bending movements to pick up the ball. And I managed to pick up six wickets before the close.'

Dark mutterings about 'shamateurs' abounded. 'There were rumours that some amateurs did get "behind-the-back' handouts,' as he put it with the utmost delicacy in *The Long Run*. 'Whether this was so I don't know, but it does remind me of one occasion during the Second World War [when I was] on a sports panel quiz with Lord Tennyson, C.B. Fry and Sir Stanley Rous. A question came up as to the difference between the amateur and the professional games player. I simply said one can afford to play for nothing, the other plays for a living. Lord Tennyson then stood up and thrusting his right-hand palm uppermost out in front of him, said the professional takes it this way, then putting his arm behind his back with the palm still uppermost, turned to Fry and, with a huge grin on his face, said, "And we took it this way, didn't we Charlie?" There was an eminent protest of denial from Charles Fry which brought laughter from the audience.'

Lord Tennyson, Lionel to all and sundry, was Alf's captain on his only major tour, to India in 1937. 'What a character. I can see him now, the day they opened the Brabourne Stadium in Bombay, in his Ascot-style tailcoat and topper. Lord Brabourne was there, the Governor. We were a bit nonplussed when Lionel insisted on playing in the match, against the Indian Universities: he'd been suffering from a nasty attack of dysentery. I can see him walking up and down, prodding the pitch and saying, "I will get a hundred on this pitch". And so he did. I liked old Lionel. Larger than life. Found dead in his bed: evening paper by his side, seven winners marked off.'

And then there was that standard-bearer for Australian aspiration, Donald George Bradman, the irresistible force who only once met anything bearing even a passing resemblance to an immoveable object. 'Cricket was the means whereby the adolescent Australia could prove its worth,' attested Charles Williams in *Bradman*, his award-winning biography of the diminutive icon. 'Cricketing heroes were its Davids and the British Empire its Goliath.' Which brings us, inevitably, to bodyline, leg theory, dignify it how you will: for all the upsetments over bumpers, beamers, bribery and tampering, no episode in the game's history can match it for amorality. Deployed, ostensibly, as a means of curbing the greatest batsman the game has ever seen (and is ever likely to see), it had a dual purpose: Britain wanted to reassert its place in the new world order and was doing everything it could to put these pesky colonials in their place, even to the extent of calling in bank loans at the height of the Depression.

According to Alf's testimony, Larwood himself seems to have had more of a creative input than is generally recognised. 'Notts tried it out against Surrey. Andy Sandham was a great hooker but Larwood and Bill Voce kept feeding him. I had a pint with Harold in the pavilion at the close – we couldn't go to the pub because we weren't allowed to be seen drinking in public – and I asked him why he and Bill had bowled so badly at Andy. "We're trying something out," he explained. "But you're getting hammered out of sight," I said. "Well," he said, "Mr Jardine knows that last time we were in Australia, whenever I bowled on leg stump in the nets he moved out of the way. So I decided the way was to follow him, and place more fielders on the leg side."

'Harold was a quiet chap but we always got on well. Against Notts on another occasion, I was summoned in a panic from the bath to go in as nightwatchman. I was in no state really and Harold immediately hit me in the box. So I went up the wicket and told him, "Easy Harold, they've dragged me out of the bath." So he said sorry and bowled the next few well outside off.

'I was once asked to bowl leg theory in a charity match down at Cardiff, by Jardine. I refused. I'd just retired but the game was being organised by a wealthy businessman and he offered me a lot of money. Their bowlers got after Jardine but they were wasting their time. He never hooked. Just got out the way. And he made ninety-odd. I liked him. He was fair enough with me. Used to say things to get me going. One time he said: "You're not trying". That's the worst thing you could accuse me of. "Bloody well bowl yourself," I told him – and walked off. Andy Sandham ran after me. "Alfred, Alfred, what are you doing?" "You heard 'im," I said. "He can bloody well bowl himself." "You're being a fool to yourself," said Andy. So I went on bowling, and ended up with five or six wickets. At the end of the day Jardine said: "Well bowled Alfred, have a drink with me". So I said: "I accept your congratulations but I don't want to have a drink with you" – and walked out. After that he was very good. As long as you stood up to him you were all right.'

Not that Alf never inflicted pain. 'I once hit George Gunn with an accidental beamer. Slipped out. He went to hook, missed, and got a fearful blow on the head. He knew it was an accident and told me so; the doctor said that if it had hit him an inch higher it would have killed him. Happliy he soon recovered, but that was certainly a factor in his decision to retire at the end of that season. I'm not against helmets, although I do think it's a farce when you see nine, ten and jack coming out with them. I never bowled a bouncer to a tailender.

'There was also an amateur fella, army captain, played for Essex. It was only just short, hit him in the teeth. They took him off, blood all over the place. "It wasn't your fault," the umpire at my end assured me. "He should have played back." I went to the dressing-room to see him. Stephenson. Colonel Stephenson – that's it. "Not your fault," he told me through broken teeth. "Should've played back." Before this, as he was being helped off, Errol Holmes, our captain, a true Corinthian, had begun waving us off. He was injured at the time so I remonstrated with Bob Gregory, his deputy, saying that we only needed one wicket to win and, as the captain on the field, it was his decision, not Errol's. We still came off, so I went straight to Errol's room to voice my protests, reminding him I'd bowled my socks off all day to get us into this position. "Alfred," he responded, "we cannot possibly win a match under these circumstances – it just isn't on."'

The most treasured delivery? No hesitation, plenty of deviation. The victim was that consummate New South Welsh stylist, Alan Kippax, Surrey v Australians, 1934. Alf claims it came back a foot or so; Kippax reckoned it was more like a yard. 'The writers called me "a fast away-swinger with an occasional breakback", but when I achieved the latter it was unintentional. It probably resulted from putting too much body into my action and keeping the seam upright instead of pointing it towards first slip. This one must have hit the seam just right. I pitched it at least twelve inches outside off stump and knocked it out as Alan padded up. "This fella bowled the best damn ball that was ever bowled to me," he said to his companion when we met up again in Australia in '54–55, by which time he had a sports shop in Sydney. I assured him it was a complete fluke. "You're too modest, Alf," he insisted, "too modest."

'Although he was a great player, I didn't mind bowling to The Don. Got him out too, though I don't remember the specifics. Played golf out in Australia with him once. "We used to reckon you, y'know," he said. "Don't know why they didn't play you." I was left out at the last minute a few times but the war did for me. A lot of people didn't like bowling at him but I told him I didn't mind. "I know that," he said.

'Patsy Hendren was harder to bowl to. Great hooker. I bounced him once, early on in my career, and he hit me for six into the Mound Stand at Lord's. Then I bowled another and he hit me for four. At the end of the over Jack [Hobbs] came up to me and asked me why I was bowling short to him. "Well," I said, "he's backing away." "He's Irish, you know," said Jack. "He kisses the Blarney Stone. Don't you believe all that – he's the best player of fast bowling in the world." "Better than you?" I replied. "Much better," he said. So a bit later Patsy asked me when I was going to bowl another short one. "You've had your ration," I said. He was a dreadful coach, apparently. Used to tell the Sussex players, "Hit it, boy, hit it harder". He was a very instinctive player, which is probably why he couldn't coach.'

ALF, FORTUNATELY, COULD coach. Which is partly why, in 1938, he bought Strudwick's share of the school co-owned since its construction ten years earlier by Sandham and, until his death in 1937, by Alf's father-in-law, W.H. (Bill) Brooke. Sandham followed 'Struddy' into retirement in 1946, leaving Alf in charge; in 1954 he purchased the premises from the trustees of the estate of his wife and sister-in-law, simultaneously picking up the lock-up garage and 'big house next door', taking the outlay to a comparatively piffling £18,000 ('Sold it at the height of the property boom a few years ago, so you can imagine how much I made').

Which is why, despite having lost his sinecure in the building trade, he felt able to retire in 1947. Having just claimed 100 wickets in a season for the eighth time, he could hardly be said to have been in terminal decline. 'Surrey had a habit of getting rid of old players, giving 'em a fortnight's notice, and I wasn't going to let that happen to me.' How could he not have been forewarned by the treatment meted out to dear old Percy George? While PGH was changing after pre-season nets at Lord's in 1936, he was joined by Errol Holmes, Surrey's 'Corinthian' captain. 'Have you thought about which two or three matches you might want to play this season?' asked Holmes. 'Do you mean you only want me for a couple of games?' retorted Fender, taken utterly unawares. 'I think so,' replied Holmes. 'In that case,' Fender jabbed back, 'I don't see any point in playing at all.'

Alf's devotion to Surrey CCC cannot be questioned. He would subsequently serve the club as chairman or member of sundry committees (Junior Cricket Committee, Senior Cricket Committee, Public Relations Committee) and, in 1980, as president, the first professional to be so honoured. Nevertheless, a distinct if gentle smirk of satisfaction settles briefly on his lips as he recalls the day he got his retaliation in first. 'We went to the Kingston Festival and there was an evening paper billboard saying "Alf Gover Retires", blah blah blah. Somebody, the captain or secretary, came up to me and said "What's this?" So I said I was packing up. "You didn't say anything," he said. "Why should I?" I replied. So he asked me why I was packing up. "I'm packing up before you pack me up," I said. They weren't going to do that to *me*.'

Not that the thirst had been entirely slaked. 'I had offers from various Lancashire League clubs – I'd played up there for Royston in 1945 – but that meant staying up there to coach the members in the evenings. The Birmingham League only required me for Saturday afternoons, for games, so I accepted an offer from West Bromwich Dartmouth, who were affiliated to West Bromwich Albion FC. Had three great years there: having failed to contend for years, we won the championship in my first two years and finished close runners-up in 1950. Drove up and back on a Saturday: played nine holes then went out to bowl. Broke the League record for wickets in a season in my first year. It was a lower standard, although I did struggle with Royston at first because I pitched a fraction too short. The crowds were like football crowds. In away games they'd boo me all the time. I found it quite amusing.

'Our batting was weak, so I acquired the services of Jim Workman, a wicket-keeper-batsman who'd played against me for the Australian Dominions in the Victory Test I played in 1945: Cec Pepper hit me for the winning runs, as I recall. Jim coached for me at weekends for twenty-four years, until his untimely death from a heart attack. He'd taken his English bride to Australia and married her but he'd come back to settle here in 1949. The thing was, each team in the League was only supposed to have one professional, and there were complaints. "Well, if you can prove we're paying Jim, then fair do's," was the club's stance – but nobody could.'

What Alf omits to mention, typically, is the part of the story that reflects best on him. Soon after Jim Workman's return to Blighty, Alf introduced him to an Australian acquaintance of his who happened to run a business in Covent Garden, on whose staff Jim would remain for the next twenty-six years. But then that's Alf. Nor did he mention those decades of charity work and fundraising with the Lord's Taverners, nor that in 1974 he became the first cricketer to be elected president of that esteemed body (he was still arranging games in the Algarve in his eighties). But then that's Alf, too. Never one to turn a good deed into an act of heroism.

Chapter 2:
The Batsman's Tale

'There is a time in the growth of some political beliefs when they so offend against common morals that they are recognisable as evil and obnoxious to right-thinking people ... I cannot believe that any gentlemen on the other side of the house would happily have played a round of golf with Hitler or Goering ...'

John Arlott, speaking against the motion 'That politics should not intrude on sporting contacts', a televised debate at the Cambridge Union, 1968

AUGUST is here, dragging in summer by the scruff of its reluctant neck. West Kirby's keenest churchgoer is entertaining a faithless Semite in his sun lounge while his charming better half rustles up some coronation chicken sandwiches. Strewn around are countless books and magazines – The Independent, Church Times, *a biography of Octavia Hill, Alan Wilkinson's* Dissent Or Conform – War, Peace and the English Churches 1900–45. *Nestling in a cassette case are recordings of Rachmaninov and Bartok. Not the most obvious accoutrements one might expect to find in the home of an ex-England cricket captain. Then again, the Rt Rev. Lord David Stuart Sheppard is hardly your common-or-garden ex-England cricket captain.*

Pop into the Lord's Museum, check out the England team photo snapped at The Oval in 1956 and it won't take long to arrive at the conclusion that here, without a glimmer of doubt, was a man at one remove. There he is, sitting at the front but off to the side on the extreme left: knees jutting out, right foot splayed, out of step with the rest. He is also the only one smiling *and* displaying his teeth. 'If he gets a half-volley, he cracks it with full swing of the bat,' Tony Lock, who stands to vague attention in the back row, once marvelled. 'Perhaps because there is more things to him in life than cricket, he is able to go through with his strokes with less concern about the consequences.'

The 'more things' in question were the poor, the homeless and the ne'er-do-wells. As Bishop of Woolwich, and later Liverpool, David Sheppard embraced Christianity as a means of helping those less fortunate. It also gave him the conviction to stand up for his beliefs where others shrugged. In 1960 he refused to play ball with the South Africans. As the first British sportsman to take a stand against the century's most abhorrent regime, part-timer or no, he occupies a lofty plinth in the pantheon.

Interviewed by Rowland Ryder for an article on Christianity and cricket published in the 1970 *Wisden*, he outlined how the game had helped forge his attitudes towards his fellow man, broadening his outlook, removing the blinkers. 'It was through cricket that I began the process of learning to respect other men for what they are and not for the colour of their skin or for the school they went to. Living for the last fourteen years in inner London – Islington, Canning Town and now Peckham – that process has been accelerated. I hope that I have learnt much more to meet all people on level terms. More than ever I believe that Christ calls in question all our attitudes and actions. If God is the God of all the earth, there can be no dividing our life into compartments which we label "sacred" and "secular".'

'DO YOU THINK you can learn to hate these Australians for the next six months?'

Thus did a senior England player spell out what was required when David first docked in Australia at the outset of the Fifties. His astonishment at the time suggests he made the right career decision. As does the tale he tells of the time Freddie Brown, the bluff character who represented, captained, selected and managed England teams for more than three decades, responded to comments about the ethics of going into a Test against Australia with Tony Lock, a terrific spinner but a convicted chucker. 'In pursuit of the urn,' he proclaimed, 'anything goes.' Would Brown (who was actually on Jardine's tour) have gone so far as to bowl bodyline? Pausing for optimum effect, he replied: 'I wouldn't have set the same field.'

It is easy, nevertheless, to forget how heroic a name David might have made for himself on the field had he not become distracted. At twenty, he won his county cap; at twenty-one, while still studying history at Cambridge (at that juncture his sights were firmly on a barrister's silks), he made his Test debut and went on an Ashes tour; at twenty-four he led Sussex to second in the championship, matching their highest high; at twenty-five he was leading his country, the youngest so to do for more than quarter of a century. He might even have attained immortality as one of only three England skippers this century to retrieve the Ashes in Australia but for one of the few recorded instances of selectorial contrition.

Hugged to the breast of the amateur establishment, who saw him as one of their own, David was prevailed upon to make himself available to command the 1954–55 expedition, even though he had by now given up full-time flanneled foolery to train for the ministry. If he was loth to miss two terms in his final year of theological studies, it also pained him to put himself up as some dilettante rival to the unmistakeably professional incumbent Len Hutton, the friend at whose memorial service he would preach four decades later, the player he most esteemed. Still, it was too enticing to resist. In fact, he made it plain, and with nary a whiff of arrogance, that he would only go in that capacity. It was, he reasons, 'a completely different contribution to make than simply going as a team member'. For the second and third Tests against Pakistan he deputised for the thirty-eight-year-old Hutton, mentally and physically drained after a torrid tour of the Caribbean: the tension did not make for an enjoyable baptism. In the event, before rain ravaged the second game, Hutton got the nod. 'I breathed a sigh of relief when I was out of it after that match,' David would reveal to Peter May's biographer, Alan Hill, some forty years later. A few days before the party was announced, one of the selectors, Walter Robins, contacted him to confirm the reason for the change of tack: 'I feel we have been very unfair to Len.'

David encountered graciousness of another hue when he made his bow for Sussex in 1947, that sumptuous summer of Compton, Edrich and all that free-form jazz. Though born in Reigate, the family had moved to their holiday retreat in Slinford when David's father, a London solicitor, died in 1937. The leggy, long-striding Sherborne schoolboy had grown a full foot after he was sixteen. He was afforded the most magnanimous of introductions. 'There'll be a run on the off side if you want it,' whispered Les Berry, the Leicestershire skipper, as David shuffled out after tea to resume his second innings, cowed by a first-innings first-baller and still on a pair. The fielders duly retreated, enabling him to push a single. As it transpired, he added just one more run.

A more salutary insight was supplied by the West Indians at Fenners in 1950, his freshman year at Trinity Hall. Opening on one of Cyril Coote's characteristically plump feather mattresses, he marched to 227 out of a stand of 343 with his chum John Dewes (with whom he would subsequently add 349 that same season, against Sussex to boot; another observant Christian, the slim Dewes would also enter a more cerebral profession, in his case teaching). Those canny little pals o' mine, Ramadhin and Valentine, shortly to mesmerise the best England had to offer with their subtly-spun variations (especially so in the care of the former, who finally confessed, almost half a century later, that he had been a chucker), were reduced to waiters, serving up one tasty morsel after another. 'At no time was this cricket one would expect from undergraduates against Test match bowlers,' attested Michael Melford in the *Telegraph*. David was duly awarded his blue after the match, albeit not before the opposition, undaunted by the unseasonal chills, had muscled their way to 730 for three. 'The real lesson we received was from [Everton] Weekes,' David told Alan Hill, awe intact. 'Cutting and hooking anything short with tremendous power, very quick to skip up the wicket to drive the slow bowlers, and driving in all directions off the back foot, which I had never really seen done before, he massacred our bowlers.'

Later that same eventful season David was on the wrong end of another milestone. Playing for The Rest against England on a track considered dodgy even by Bradford's indecent standards (it had been soaked after being left uncovered for the day before the match), he was one of eight victims claimed by Jim Laker in exchange for two measly runs – still the most statistically destructive analysis in *Wisden*. 'And I'll tell you what, if Godfrey Evans hadn't brought off a simply stunning stumping to get rid of Fred Trueman off Alec Bedser, it would have been *nine* for two.' Not that any of this prevented another 2,000-run haul.

Nineteen fifty-one saw Hutton acquire his hundredth hundred and Sussex emerge as one of only two counties with a trading profit. A benefit for one of

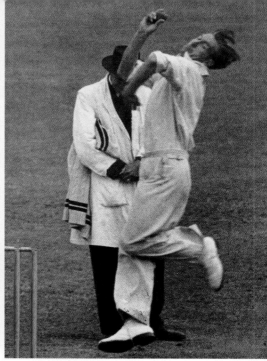

Above left: A bottle of suave... a dapper-looking Alf in his prime, 1938 (*Hulton Getty*); above right: Pacing himself... once notorious for the length of his run, Alf trimmed his approach and prolonged a career that in 1936 saw him become the first English fast bowler to take 200 wickets in a season for 39 years. He repeated the feat the very next summer, the last of his breed to do so (*Hulton Getty*)
Below: Khan do... Andy Sandham, former owner of the cricket school Alf would buy outright a year later, looks on approvingly as Alf passes on some pearls, 1953 (*from left*): Sandham, Rosi Dinshaw, Imtiaz Ahmed, Alf, Khan Mohammad and Agar Sadaj. Imtiaz and Khan 'showed outstanding ability' and went on to help Pakistan draw their Test series in England the following year (*Sport and General*)

Overleaf: Still twinkling... Alf in his bedroom, June 1998 (*Graham Goldwater*)

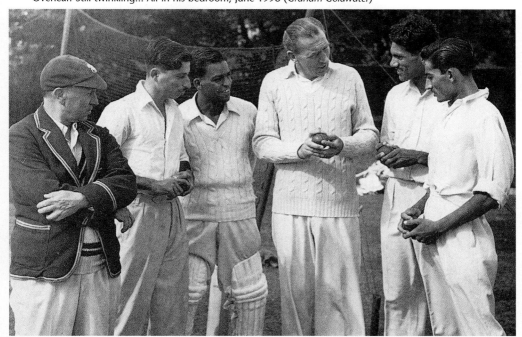

their stoutest servants, George Cox, raked in £6620; Alec Bedser was advertising Ovaltine 'at 1/6, 2/6 and 4/6'. David led the Hove averages with 1142 runs at 57; his final tally again exceeded 2000, including seven centuries. 'Sheppard produced his best and most brilliant form when he became available,' enthused Jack Arledge, that sweetly venerable mine host of the Hove press box, 'revealing batsmanship of a maturity and class that marked him out as a player of true England standard. His 67 against Yorkshire on a turning wicket at Hove must rank as about the finest innings of the summer.' The next season he led Cambridge, breaking all Light Blue records with 1281 runs and another septet of centuries (including his side's first in the Varsity match since the war), finishing with the most runs compiled for Cambridge to date, 3545. He also topped the national averages ahead of the purportedly more gifted P.B.H. May. Humility and realism collide as he plays down such apparent precocity.

'I think England were struggling to get going again after the war. We'd lost half a generation. The selectors were casting about. I don't think I was quite good enough to play Tests at twenty-one. I don't think I was good enough to play for Sussex at eighteen. What was good for me was that I realised that there was a standard that you have to go for and not give up on. We were certainly struggling when I went to Australia the first time. Denis [Compton] began to have dreadful trouble with his knee, and averaged seven-point-something in the Tests. Lost all his confidence. Cyril Washbrook wasn't the opener he was; the Australians thought they could bounce him out, and did. So the selectors picked a clutch of young batsmen: myself, Parkhouse, Dewes and Close. We all struggled.

'It was an object lesson for me. On the boat out I'd badgered and badgered Len [Hutton] to talk to me but he kept trying to brush me off. Eventually he took me under his wing but when we arrived in Perth I was still badgering him. The WACA pitch was very fast for our first match, and West Australia had a fast bowler named Charlie Puckett. The top joint of my thumb is still thicker than it should be, from the blow from a lifting delivery from Puckett. I battled it out for fifty minutes at the start of the innings and was then out for a single-figure score. When I came off Len said: "Well batted". I looked suspiciously at him. "No, I mean it," he said. "You've made it easy for the others." Later, Brian Close went in at number seven, took all sorts of chances, had a lot of good luck, and scored a century. When he came off, Len gave him a terrific dressing-down for not learning from his mistakes and building a sound innings. I learned something from that. As a captain, I always said you should never shout at someone who's made nought. It's much more constructive to have a go at someone who has made runs, and thrown his wicket away by doing something silly.'

Not that that was the limit of his admiration for Hutton, who held up the England order on that trip much as a copper might prop up a drunk. 'I came back under the influence. Until then I was a typical public school, inside-out, off-side player. Andy Sandham had taught me how to hook when I was nine, in the days when he and Alf Gover ran Alf's school. But when I watched Len play a defensive shot it never went on the off-side; always straight back. I took it all in but the following summer I couldn't hit a ball on the off-side. I'd got the off-side back by 1952 and that was the first time I felt ready to play for England. But then just before a Test in 1957 I jarred my left hand. For a party piece I had learned to imitate Len's batting. Because he had broken his left arm during the war, his left arm was shortened, and he held his top hand at the back of the bat handle rather than at the front. So, with my jarred hand, I batted in the Test quite successfully, doing my Hutton imitation.

'The first time I faced Lindwall and Miller was against New South Wales in Sydney. Len made a hundred and I came in for the second new ball, 200 for two or whatever. It was bouncer, yorker, bouncer, yorker, bouncer, yorker – four bouncers in an eight-ball over. The "full treatment", that's what they called it. I always said bodyline was the worst thing in cricket, the most wicked thing, but that wasn't pleasant either. I'd seen photos of Len sitting down on the wicket with his bat over his head after Lindwall and Miller had bounced him out in '46–47 and '48, and now he was doing it again. The best thing is if both sides have a couple of genuinely fast bowlers: that way bowlers think twice about trying to knock someone's head off.' Unfortunately for the poor abused batsman, this has rarely, if ever, been the case. In 1981, England's riposte to Roberts, Holding, Garner and Croft was Dilley, Botham, Jackman and Gooch, which is a bit like tackling the SAS with a toothpick.

Recalled in 1956 on one of Gubby Allen's inspired whims, David made an invaluable 113 in 'Laker's Match' at Old Trafford, stirring E.W. Swanton to laud his 'handsome and powerful strokes'. Ian Johnson, the Australian captain, was impressed on a different count. 'It is not unusual for players in the heat of contact to use various expletives. Tony Lock [was] one ... so too [was] I. Yet when David came into the England team even Tony restrained himself. I did, too. If he has that effect on hard-bitten sportsmen, his effect on the young must be very much greater.' Not that Lock could completely suppress his propensity for animated oath-flinging. After stumps one day, David hastened to the visitors' dressing room to apologise for his colleague's indiscretions.

IN TRUTH, ENGLISH cricket could afford to lose David to the church. The quality of Her Majesty's batsmanship in that last decade of domination – or rather, the irresistibility of her bowlers – meant he was seldom missed. Bit by bit he disappeared from the scene, literally and figuratively. His entry in the *Playfair Who's Who* for 1952 began: 'RHB with admirable technique and range. Versatile field – grand short leg.' By 1955 it was 'Outstanding RHB who is also one of the safest close fields in the country.' Come 1957 the 'outstanding' had gone.

That summer brought two outings against the West Indies (68 at Leeds, 40 at The Oval – in those days England could still beat them by an innings) but priorities lay elsewhere: with his new bride, the aptly-named Grace, and his duties as warden of the Mayflower Centre, tending to the disadvantaged youths of London's East End. He continued to spend his annual month at Sussex, still piercing the covers with eager felicity, the notion of a Test recall submerged but not entirely discounted. In 1960, the Duke of Norfolk invited him, as was his wont, to captain his XI at Arundel in the annual tour pipe-opener. Only that year the tourists were South Africa. 'I knew that I was not willing to play against an all-white team representing South Africa. The big question for me was whether I should keep my objections to myself, or go public with my refusal.

'Apartheid drew cricket into one of the great issues of humanity, and a great issue of justice for the Christian Church. I knew that Black Christians all over Africa were being taunted that Christianity was just a white man's trick to maintain white supremacy. South Africa claimed to be the most Christian country in the world. The motivation for me in going public was to say, "here's at least one Christian who can't be a part, *won't* be a part of that system". I had asked advice of several clergy in South Africa. One had said that he did not think Christians should get involved in politics but the others all encouraged me to speak up. At the time I was a member of the MCC Committee, who in a real sense were the hosts for the tour. I asked the president, Harry Altham, if I could explain my motives to the committee. One of the older members, Col R.T. Stanyforth, protested furiously, saying that this was political, and quite improper. Harry rebuked him, and said I had a perfect right to explain what was a matter of conscience.

'BBC News came down to the Mayflower to interview me. I had flu. I knew this would be at the top of the News. I remember telling myself, "Don't go on speaking, once you have said what you intend to say – don't give them any more rope". I made the point I needed to do in a minute, and said no more. I had crossed the Rubicon.'

Fast-forward to 1968 and the D'Oliveira Affair. Wherein a gifted and genial Cape Coloured all-rounder, denied a suitable living in his inhumane homeland, finds himself signed by Worcestershire at the urging of that renowned humanitarian John Arlott, forces his way into the England team then metamorphoses into the bounciest political football ever to grace a field. Without Basil D'Oliveira the sports boycott that gnawed at white South Africa's notions of manhood might never have happened. And without that boycott ...

He would never describe it as such himself, of course, but, to the public at least, it became David's *cause célèbre*. 'I think I was a bit out of sympathy with cricket by then. I was still on the MCC cricket committee, which had become less and less powerful. At the start of the tour of the West Indies, for which Dolly was selected but didn't do terribly well, I raised the question: are we taking any steps to ensure South Africa will accept any team we sent there the following winter? There were a lot of blank faces and probably some red ones.' It was around this time, in March, that Sir Alec Douglas-Home flew out for a word with John Vorster, the South African premier. He concluded that there would be no objections to D'Oliveira and conveyed this confidence when he returned.

The next few chapters are engraved in cricket's Doomsday Book. D'Oliveira retains his place for the opening Test against Australia, scores 87 in an otherwise pitiful second-innings collapse and is expeditiously dropped, ostensibly in favour of a third specialist seamer. As he relates in his autobiography, however, 'A high-ranking official told me on the eve of the Lord's Test that I could get everyone out of trouble by making myself available for South Africa, not England. I angrily refused.' Whereupon Tiene Oosthuizen, UK managing director of the Carreras Tobacco Company, meets him in London and throws an enticing offer on the table: £4000 per annum for the next ten years 'with a car, house and generous expenses thrown in', to coach coloured South Africans. The one proviso is that he declare himself unavailable for the impending tour by England, still trading overseas under the MCC banner. Oosthuizen, furthermore, claims to have it on the highest possible authority that D'Oliveira's presence on the Veldt in an MCC blazer would be intensely embarrassing to the home government and that he could depend on being declared *persona non grata*. D'Oliveira decides this is all 'far too fishy'. Mystified and disenchanted with his continued exclusion from the Test squad, however, he tells his suitor he cannot make a decision until the announcement of the winter party, scheduled for the day after the final Test. Suddenly, by some freakish chain of injury and happenstance, he receives an eleventh-hour summons to The Oval, survives five presentable chances (the Gods really were working overtime on this one) and tosses off a thundering, series-levelling 158.

David was holed up in Belgium. 'The Mayflower had taken a family party to Blankenberg, which is the same as pretending you're going abroad because it's just like Southend. There were about a hundred of us in a cheap hotel and we had crises all day long. The last thing I was thinking about was cricket.

Grace had been listening to the midnight news when I came into our bedroom and had heard that Dolly had not been selected. She told me, and I didn't sleep a wink for wondering what I should do.

'I caught a plane back to England and gave myself two or three days clear before I was needed back at the Mayflower. I was determined to find out what had happened. At first I was given the official line: he hadn't had a very good tour of the West Indies; he couldn't bowl a hoop downhill. Next I went to Lord's where a big match was going on. John Arlott was there. He told me that I should know "that there was a letter". I went into the Pavilion and sat next to the journalist and broadcaster Neil Durden-Smith. I was casting about for possible allies. I wondered whether anyone connected with Worcestershire might want to take up the cudgels on Dolly's behalf. "Do you think Charles Cobham might be interested?" I asked. I had forgotten that Neil had been Lord Cobham's ADC when he was Governor-General of New Zealand. So I rang Charles up, and asked if I might come and see him. He was wildly indiscreet. As a former President of MCC and premier viscount of England, he told me he had visited South Africa that spring, had a private interview with Mr Vorster, and asked the crucial question – would Dolly be accepted, if he was selected. Vorster's reply had been that anyone else would be accepted but not D'Oliveira. When Tom Cartwright dropped out of the party, Dolly was selected. Mr Vorster then said that the team was not the team of the MCC but of the Anti-Apartheid Movement, and declared that the tour was off.'

Thus did David come to see the MCC committee as the secondary villains of the piece (though imbeciles seems a more appropriate description). Had Cobham's report simply been laughed off in light of Douglas-Home's assurances – or were there other, more sinister forces afoot? 'Somebody put a message in *The Guardian* saying "are there any other MCC members as appalled as I am?" The upshot was a dozen of us gathered in this little flat in north-west London, and out of that came a remarkable little group. We went through fire together, and developed a deep trust for one another. I was at the sharp end because I was the only major cricket name associated with the group, until Mike Brearley joined us. We called for a Special General Meeting of the MCC.

'The secretary of the MCC was Billy Griffith, who did more than anyone to introduce me to the game, who cared deeply about it. He saw a lot of things the way we did. He'd been appalled by what he'd seen in South Africa in '48–49. If he had not been in that post I always thought he would have joined our protesting group. He was deeply unhappy about the row. He felt his beautiful game was being harmed. He and I met on a number of occasions to talk about our request for a Special General Meeting. Our communications weren't very clear, I suppose, so that, when four of our group went to Lord's, thinking we were going to meet a similar small group to plan the Meeting on a civilised basis, we found that the full MCC committee had been summoned to meet with us.

'They included Sir Alec Douglas-Home, the former Prime Minister, who said he had flown down specially from Scotland to be present. They tried to persuade us to call off our request. Sir Alec kept saying: "You can't ask these people hypothetical questions." I knew, but couldn't say, that they *had* been asked the question, and that some at least in the MCC circle knew what the answer was. Eventually, Gubby Allen, who was in the chair, said: "You may as well know that we did write, asking if any team we selected would be given the usual courtesies. We never received a reply." So I believed that they had taken the terrible risk of not insisting on a reply, and perhaps hoping that, if Dolly's poor form on the West Indies tour continued, the issue would never arise.

'The Special General Meeting was the most fraught that I have ever attended. Mike Brearley and I had gone to his father's house beforehand, to run through our speeches. I would propose the vote of censure and Mike would second it. We said we mustn't indulge in personalities – don't attack anyone. The joke, of course, was that it was being held in Church House.

'There were a few cracks, and various bitter words, aimed at me, I suppose because I was the one visible target. At one juncture, Mike, who was sitting next to me, turned his body round as if to shield me. There was one bit of humour. One lugubrious old member got up and made a bitter attack on me which went on and on. "I don't know how the Bishop of Woolwich can wear his MCC tie," he said, whereupon a bloke in the gallery piped up: "Down the back". We lost the vote but we got a very large number, much more than we'd expected. I don't think there's much doubt that the argument turned and turned from that point.

'Dolly came to see me in Liverpool some years later. He had come to hold very strong views about racial discrimination in South African cricket. At the time of the controversy, I think he felt he could not speak, because he was very grateful to English cricket for giving him an opportunity to play. You know the old quote from him, of course. Asked what it felt like to win his first cap for England, he replied: "I sleep with it, man."'

Almost inevitably, the ruckus cost David a friendship. 'The group met up again at our house to try and mend fences where we could. We invited Billy Griffith, who came. I also invited Peter May, a close friend from Cambridge days. Sadly, he replied: "I don't think we've got anything to talk about". Peter had some close links with South African cricket, having captained an England tour there, and having Harold Gilligan as his father-in-law, who was South Africa's representative on the International Cricket Conference. Peter played cricket in the best possible spirit, but as others have commented, if he took up a stance he could be very hard, very unyielding.

'The following year, 1970, South Africa was due to tour England. The rugby union tour the previous winter had seen many protests. I had joined one of them, outside Twickenham. As the cricket tour drew nearer, the Stop the Tour campaign, with Peter Hain as its leader, made their plans. They included talk of flashing mirrors in the batsmen's eyes. I went to one of their meetings, and argued that they should confine their protests to outside the ground. It was plain that they continued to think of major disruptions.

'A number of us then formed the Fair Cricket Campaign. We were absolutely opposed to the tour going ahead, but did not agree with the tactics of the Stop the Tour campaign. I was the chair. Edward Boyle, Conservative minister, and Reg Prentice, then a Labour MP, were vice chairs. The secretary was one Betty Boothroyd. Edward Boyle was particularly active, going to see a whole series of people in our attempts to persuade those in authority in cricket to act. One of our successes was a visit by black sixth-formers with their head-master from Kennington School to Geoffrey Howard, then secretary at The Oval. He told me how impressed he was. They told him how much they loved coming to The Oval, but that, if South Africa played there, they would have to be outside the ground, protesting. Our activities received little publicity, but I believe that short campaign had quite a lot of effect in persuading people that we could not pretend that sport could just go on as if the injustice of apartheid had nothing to do with us.'

David finally went to the Republic twenty-one years later, shortly after Ali Bacher had orchestrated his final, fateful 'rebel' tour. On one level he found vindication, on another, hope. 'By then everyone was saying the sports boy-cott was very effective, and absolutely right, even in South Africa. I wrote to Ali, asking him if he would like to show me what he was doing in the town-ships coaching scheme. He took us out to Tembise, near Johannesburg. They had covered the ground with sand, and produced a flat wicket. The young pro-fessional who drove us there went round the primary schools, coaching and selecting the most promising boys to come to the central ground that we saw. There were some uneasy feelings about. No male teachers were involved there. I told Ali that I greatly admired what he was doing, but that it was tremen-dously difficult. In England we have failed in inner city areas to establish good opportunities for boys.

'I still think they've got problems because apartheid did its work so thor-oughly and brutally. They bulldozed Sophiatown, pushed people over the hills. What you need in cricket is an unbroken chain – park, school, village, club, first-class. We have that chain at Sussex, so you know we should be better! We knew where John Snow was when he was fifteen. But what happens when a young black player wants to move on to good club cricket?

' "It'll take you a long time to achieve what you want but good luck," I said to Ali. "Oh no," he said, "we'll have a black player in the Test team in three years." It took a bit longer, of course, but to his tremendous credit he has stuck to it. It was great to be at Old Trafford a few weeks ago to see both Ntini and Adams playing, representing the whole of South Africa. It was a great thing. But, in hindsight, I have to agree with Desmond Tutu, who I admire very greatly. It was impossible to play a non-political game in South Africa. You couldn't do anything there that was non-political.'

IN AN EERIE echo of the behind-the-scenes machinations of 1954, parson returned to pitch in 1962. Once again he was sounded out with a view to leading England Down Under; once again he was urged to take a sabbatical for the greater good. This time it was a three-way tussle, opposing him two of his closest cricketing *confrères*, Colin Cowdrey and Ted Dexter. By way of adding spice to the scenario, Dexter also happened to be his county captain. All depended on their respective showings in the third week of July, in the 137th and final dust-up at Lord's between Gentlemen and Players, a match that would come to be regarded as a richly symbolic if far from belated farewell to the feudal amateur–pro distinction. When Cowdrey, due to lead the Gents, dropped out through injury, a century on the first day looked to have put David in pole position. Conviction hardened when an observant pressman, having spotted Walter Robins – yes, him again – walking beneath the dining-room, called down to the chairman of selectors, demanding to know whether 'The Rev' had landed the job. Walter hoisted both thumbs, the following morning's headlines paid excessive homage to the ecclesiastical pun – and Dexter got the nod. While Robins had evidently decided that appointing a part-timer wasn't such a sound idea after all, the smell of a hidden agenda was difficult to ignore.

'It was extraordinary. Robins virtually offered me the captaincy over the phone before the season started. He rang me up and asked me over to Gubby Allen's flat to discuss it. They wanted to press me, make certain I wouldn't talk about the Australian government's "white Australia" policy. They wanted to find out whether I was going to make trouble for them. I made a hundred in my first game, against a very poor Oxford side, and the papers got hold of that, but then I had a dreadful run. Everyone at Hove seemed to feel sad for me. I recovered but in the end Robins couldn't bring himself to tell me I hadn't got the captaincy. I only found out when Crawford White, the correspondent of the *Daily Express*, came into the dressing-room and asked me if I had any comment to make.'

Terra familiar... David Sheppard back at Hove, August 1998 (*Graham Goldwater*)

'As the bishop said to the actress'... England's leading lights share the sweetness of victory over Australia at Melbourne's MCG in 1962 (*from left*): Fred Trueman, Ted Dexter, David and Colin Cowdrey (*Sydney Morning Herald*)

Peak practice… David drives Richie Benaud, captaining Australia, to reach his matchwinning century at the MCG, 1962 (*Sydney Morning Herald*)

Below: Jury in session… the 1962–63 tour selection committee convenes at the Sydney Cricket Ground (*from left*): Cowdrey, Dexter, Duke of Norfolk, David, Brian Statham and Alec Bedser (*The Observer*)

Late date... David cuts Fazal Mahmood while captaining England against Pakistan at Trent Bridge in 1962, the leadership of an Ashes tour in the offing (*Hulton Getty*)

Grace and flavour... David and his wife Grace, another keen watcher of flanneled foolery, admire a boundary by Sussex's Rajesh Rao, Hove, August 1998 (*Graham Goldwater*)

Scarborough fare… Brian Close prospers against Middlesex, 1965, the year he led Yorkshire to their first Gillette Cup; the following year brought the first of three successive championships, the last the club has won (*Patrick Eagar*)

Grim and bear it… Brian and Colin Cowdrey at The Oval, 1967, having just been censured for purported time-wasting tactics against Warwickshire. When Brian was subsequently sacked as England captain, Cowdrey took over (*Hulton Getty*)

In contrast to 1954, having made no pre-conditions, David was happy to join the ranks, albeit as a member of the selection committee. The media swooned but one nose was thrust firmly out of joint. Already cheesed off at the attention showered on David and the manager, the Duke of Norfolk, whose passion for horses made him an instant object of Australian affection, Fred Trueman, who never did take too kindly to sharing the spotlight, aired his frustrations to a journalist when Susan Dexter, the skipper's delectable model wife, swept into town. 'I told him I was a bit confused, not knowing whether we were supposed to be playing under Jockey Club rules, for Dexter Enterprises or engaged on a missionary hunt.'

If a group of contemporary selectors were to choose an amateur, needless to say, the quantity of marbles at their disposal would be severely questioned. Yet, all things considered, David had about as bountiful a trip as could reasonably be asked of a man who hadn't concentrated on his batting for the best part of a decade.

Reactions, inevitably, were rusty, provoking some chastening moments in the field that would duly be recycled for Trueman's after-dinner repertoire. 'It all began in that Gents *v* Players match. I caught Peter Parfitt at short leg, right off the middle. Peter went back to the dressing-room, threw his bat down, and Freddie, who was captaining the Players, said: "Bad luck, Peter, the Reverend has got a better chance than most of us when he puts his hands together." Fielding was the one thing I was nervous about after nine years of irregular play. I think I'd made myself a good close-to-the-wicket catcher, but so much of that is instinctive, and that can go when you stop doing it regularly. I stood too close and dropped a couple, and once you do that your confidence starts to go. And when I dropped one off Freddie he was ready. He's dined out on his remark on the Rev needing to put his hands together, not just for prayer, ever since.'

At the crease, more grievously, the left shoulder pointed wide of mid-on, rendering him susceptible to Alan Davidson's brisk left-arm swing. He compensated with determination and patience, weapons honed in Canning Town. Coping with Richie Benaud as well as anyone ('though only after Richie had made me look very foolish in Brisbane'), he fared better in the Tests – 330 runs at 33 – than Parfitt, Pullar or Graveney. 'Had he not owed so many runs before he started, no one need have complained,' Alan Ross slyly observed in *Australia 63*. In Melbourne, moreover, he scaled rarefied heights, becoming one of the precious few Englishman with a cv boasting a match-winning century in the fourth innings of an Ashes altercation. At the bottom of the Sheppards' immaculate garden, overlooking the Wirral Way, stands an Acer Crimson King tree, a gift from Lord Cowdrey of Tonbridge to commemorate their decisive stand.

'It was an astonishing resurrection,' testified Ross. 'For four hours he played with the assurance of one who had heard an old nostalgic tune, its melody as it made itself familiar recalling forgotten and delightful associations. His stroke-play acquired a dream-like smoothness, all angularities and awkwardnesses smoothed away. When it was over he was near collapse, but the song's echoes were of the kind that linger indelibly.' Exhilarated and exhausted as he was, David was no less relieved. 'It was a match of highlights and lowlights. I made nought in the first innings, dropped one difficult catch, then dropped another off Bill Lawry, who'd been batting all day, in the last over of the day. Got my hands under it, but ... So I said to Ted, "I'm going to get into this game".

'That tour was a toughening experience for me. I'd been out of it all. I didn't think I'd play for England again. I observed much more clearly what was going on, and to see Ted, then twenty-seven, being treated as if he was a prime minister, and expected to have a full-blown press conference *every* day of a Test. Richie [Benaud], I think, instigated that. And quite relished it.'

Not that David confined himself to the crease. It was standing-room only when he addressed a congregation from the pulpit. 'He might have fared a good deal more successfully had he been allowed to concentrate solely on his cricketing duties,' noted a sympathetic Davidson, who felt that that MCG salute was the only occasion his bunny resembled his pre-Mayflower self. 'But there was no such thing as a leisure hour for [him] and he was whisked off to a multitude of church engagements. He was, of course, a magnificent symbol to place before the young people of Australia.'

BANK HOLIDAY MONDAY at Hove and the deckchairs are heaving. Lord and Lady Sheppard recline on their MCC cushions, binoculars trained. Lunch in the committee room beckons. Sixty miles to the north at The Oval, Muttiah Muralitharan is weaving his wristy sorcery, pinioning the home batsmen en route to the fifth-fattest hoard of wickets in a Test and a gleeful first win on English soil for Sri Lanka, treated so disdainfully for so long. David is more interested in the revival being orchestrated by Sussex's young gunners, gritty Rajesh Rao and clean-hitting Robin Martin-Jenkins. 'Did you see that?' he exclaims as Rao's off-drive clatters off the perimeter hoardings, a Glamorgan fielder trotting half-heartedly in its slipstream, that championship title long since surrendered. A sigh greets Rao's exit, the scorecard filled in with a measured, regretful hand. When CMJ Jr crashes a drive through extra-cover the enthusiasm is wide-eyed: a first-former reborn.

He has attended more games this summer than for many a moon. Retirement has its advantages. Not that luck has exactly pursued him. He went to two days of the Old Trafford Test against South Africa but missed England's riveting and restorative rearguard action on the Monday. He'd also been there for Sussex's first-round defeat by Lancashire in the NatWest Trophy. And he'd set up camp at Eaton Road for the previous championship fixture only to see Hampshire hare home in two days. Parochial pleasures were overdue. Every so often a chap in late middle-age sidles over clutching autograph book and camera. Every request is indulged with willing pen and broad smile.

Belonging to the last generation of English cricketers to sample success with any meaningful regularity can be a mixed blessing. Bask as you sheepishly do in the glow (having tasted defeat in his first two Tests, David endured just one more reversal in his subsequent twenty), you know full well that anything you submit as a reason for the decline is likely to be ridiculed as the foamings of a snotty old dodderer who firmly believes mankind will never, ever again have it remotely so good. The only man to play Test cricket as an ordained minister, is, as you might expect, more cautious than most. What he will do is wag a finger at the pitches.

'During my time the game here was moved into the hands of the seam bowler. My first trip to Lord's as a player was for a schools match in 1947 – I'd seen Bradman bat there in '38, only for my hero, Hedley Verity, to disappoint me by bowling him for 18. Nineteen forty-seven was a very dry summer. The ball bumped across a parched outfield and the shine was knocked off in no time. They still put marl on the wicket: it was like standing in red dust. That produced a fast wicket which would turn at the end of the match. The Sussex grounds were the same. Fast bowlers loved Hastings and Hove, because there was pace and the ball bounced. So did Doug Wright, because a leg-spinner could make it bounce and turn a bit. The good batsmen loved it too, because you could play strokes at the ball which came through fast. In Australia in 1950–51 as a very new Test player, I battled for a long time trying to save the match at Adelaide. Lindwall and Miller took the second new ball. After two overs Lindwall held up the ball and said "Look at that". It was like a gooseberry. You couldn't keep the shine on there. By 1957 outfields were all kept watered overnight by the new technology. Grassy outfields made it possible to keep the shine on almost indefinitely. That year I found it easier to score runs in the Tests than in county matches, where on grassy pitches the ball was always moving off the seam.'

He has obviously given the matter a fair deal of thought. Not that this should come as any surprise. Cricket always has been his favourite diversion, the most dependable escape hatch. Those alert eyes glint as he casts back to his childhood fervour. How he would while away the summer holidays during the war playing eleven-a-side, two-innings matches on his own abetted by tennis ball, bat and wall ('I couldn't see any friends because of petrol rationing so one spring I started a county championship – all play all – and during the next two or three years I got through all the matches that would have been played by the end of May'). How he assiduously memorised the mode and style of his favourite batsmen then strove to impersonate each and every one. How he had had his work cut out because he had already seen sixteen of the seventeen first-class counties in action by the time he was ten.

'I'll tell you something, if I can't get to sleep I pick world XIs based purely on the alphabet. H and B were always the best but recently the Ws have suddenly come forward. Waqar, Wasim, Warne, Waugh, Waugh.'

You can take the bishop out of the boy, but never the boy out of the bishop.

Chapter 3:
The Captain's Tale

'I was covering the Bath Festival, in the Seventies or just after. Someone called to me in the beer tent. It was Peter O'Toole, back in Bristol playing *Uncle Vanya* at Theatre Royal. We'd known each other when he was a fledgling pro actor just out of RADA. In confidential tones, this most extrovert of actors told me he had one especial wish. Would I introduce him to Brian Close, fellow Yorkshireman, then captaining Somerset, at the close? I did as I was asked. I'm not sure which of them was the more shy – or thrilled.'

David Foot, 1998

ONCE UPON A TIME there lived a group of cricket-potty friends known as the Four Yorkshiremen of the Apocalypse. Frederick was the eldest, the fearsome fast bowler, unimpeded by delusions of mortality. Geoffrey was the introspective kid with the specs, opening bat supreme, never knowingly one to put the team before Geoffrey. Raymond was an off-spinner, useful middle-order bat, canny tactician and never wittingly wrong. And then there was Dennis, eighteen days Frederick's junior, Brian to all; even his mum: another off-spinning all-rounder and canny tactician, a restless, tactless free spirit who never consciously took a backward step. Unfortunately, his intelligence and talent exceeded his concentration.

They didn't always get on. Squabbles were frequent. One morning, while they were playing a game far, far away, in the tiny kingdom of Wales, Geoffrey dropped a catch off Brian, who, unfortunately for Geoffrey, also happened to be the captain. Come lunchtime, Brian was in a rotten mood. So much so, the rest of the team fled the dressing room. All except Geoffrey, who had only recently been elevated to the first XI and was unfamiliar with Brian's famous temper. When Brian started making pointed comments about fielding standards, Geoffrey resolved to stand up for himself. 'If I'd dropped as many as you this morning ...' he began. The next thing he knew – or so he claims – Brian had him pinned against the wall, fist cocked. It was a good thing Geoffrey wasn't scared of heights, for there was now a considerable distance between his feet and the floor. Frederick and Raymond arrived in the nick of time, separating the boys just as Geoffrey's chin was on the verge of doing untold damage to Brian's knuckles.

Brian, one scarce needs add, tells the story rather differently. 'Never happened,' he insists with some vehemence. The pals also agreed to disagree on what Brian declared to be his most cherished moment as a leader of men. Brian claimed it was his prodding that encouraged Geoffrey to bat as he never had before (nor ever did again) and so win a cup final; Geoffrey accepted the plaudits but vehemently denied that he needed – or received – any coaxing. 'Brian either inspired or frightened him,' concluded one reliable witness.

Frederick, Geoffrey and Raymond grew up to be media 'experts', famed throughout the land, albeit marginally more for their wit than their wisdom. Some called them 'professional Yorkshiremen'. Brian carried more cricketing wisdom in his little toe than the other three put together, had more natural talent than the other three put together, led them all to countless triumphs. He pushed Geoffrey into opening against his wishes, restored Raymond to the national team and prolonged Frederick's bowling career. He also adored cricket so much he played professionally until his forty-seventh year and was still having the odd sortie in his sixty-eighth. 'Any mistakes I made came from putting the game first,' he declares proudly, a familiar refrain if one is to believe Geoffrey. He grew up to be shot at.

WHICH IS WHY, as we sit outside the committee bar at windswept, desolate Headingley watching Yorkshire duel with Surrey, fully thirty Septembers since he had led God's own county to its thirtieth and most recent championship, Brian Close rues the absence of a suitable public platform for his insightful and trenchant views on the innumerable self-inflicted flaws he perceives in the English game. 'I wish I'd been commentating on TV,' he barks through a haze of smoke ('smoking helps me focus my thoughts'). Those ample eyebrows unknot. He is referring to the way Muttiah Muralitharan had just taken sixteen English wickets at The Oval. 'I'd have given 'em hell. Someone ought to tell them to use their feet and hands properly.'

From where his inquisitor sits, the Life of this particular Brian is best captured, not by that irreverent Monty Python movie's oft-repeated closing ditty, 'Always Look On The Bright Side of Life', but in one by that similarly rambunctious Seventies act, The Who:

> Laugh and say I'm green
> I've seen things you'll never see
> Talk behind my back
> But I'm off the beaten track
> I'll take on anyone
> Ain't scared of a bloody nose
> Drink till I drop down
> With one eye on my clothes

Here, above all, is a man who thrives on challenges. Taking up golf, and advised by Yorkshire's senior pros that using his natural – i.e. left – hand could impair his batting, he became a right-handed, single-figure handicapper. Later, he changed back to his natural left-handed mode, and became a single-figure handicapper within a couple of months. Smitten upon meeting a BOAC hostess from Ottery St Mary at the Beach Club in Bermuda, he duly wined and dined the fair damsel that very night. 'Look, I'm sorry,' he blurted after the meal. 'I know you are engaged but *I* am going to marry you.' And so he did.

Ask his peers about Brian's most compelling attribute and they concur to a man. Courageous? Put it this way, if Medusa, Godzilla and King Kong joined forces, they'd be doing the cowering. Yet it was that very fearlessness, touched as it could be with fecklessness, that undid him – on two fronts. As a player it denied him a more glittering career in football and, as a by-product, diminished the capabilities that had once seemed destined to make him the nation's most redoubtable all-round cricketer since Wally Hammond (and confine Trevor Bailey to a career at Essex). Had his concentration span been longer, who knows: he might have left Botham for dead. As it was, in twenty-two Tests spanning twenty-seven years, he never passed 70 and only against India did he glean more than two wickets. He found his metier as captain, a task for which his boundless selflessness and self-belief equipped him admirably. He consummated it with uncommon ardour and acumen. Sadly, it was that selfsame dauntlessness, that disdain for compromise, which ultimately robbed him of the honours he had so richly earned: leadership of county and country. That CBE was scant consolation.

Herewith some testimonies from the other members of that apocalyptic (and not infrequently apoplectic) quartet.

'The appointment of Brian Close as captain of Yorkshire met with [Fred's] approval,' attested John Arlott, biographer of Frederick Trueman OBE. Need we say more? 'Everyone who has ever had any dealings with Dennis Brian Close has a love–exasperation relationship,' warranted Raymond Illingworth CBE, boyhood pal, best man, bridge partner and trustiest onfield adviser. 'We all know his faults but I can't think of anyone who doesn't forgive him for them … If he is your friend he is a staunch and loyal friend. He is godfather to my elder daughter Vicky and he never [failed] to arrive to see her on Christmas Eve. When I had to tell him to get stuffed he would take it from me when he wouldn't have taken it from anyone else. I was very happy to serve under him. It was a good side … a happy side … a winning side … a well-led side … when he was attacking there was not a better captain anywhere …'

'[Brian] was the epitome of the way Yorkshire play cricket. Strong and positive, a bit bloody-minded perhaps, but a man who left nobody in doubt that our job was to win matches … He had more influence on my attitudes, and even aptitudes, than anyone else … His sacking [by Yorkshire] must still rank as one of the cruellest incidents in the history of sport.' Thus spake the man who profited, Geoffrey Boycott OBE, quite possibly the least temperamentally and philosophically equipped candidate to succeed *any* captain, let alone the one and only D.B. Close.

That fateful, unpopular and hotly divisive decision jump-started a series of public spats that would see English cricket's proudest institution descend into a brand of internecine warfare that made the Montagues and Capulets seem like The Waltons. Fading dynasties always do eat their own. Boycott dispatched

Where the heart is… Brian on the committee-room balcony, Headingley, September 1998
(*Graham Goldwater*)

Return to arms… England's youngest-ever Test player sweeps against the West Indies at Lord's in 1976, having been recalled at 45 (*Patrick Eagar*)

Sacrificial lion… Brian, thrust into the firing line as opener to protect the young Bob Woolmer, allows himself to be hit by a bouncer from Michael Holding amid the Old Trafford gloaming, 1976 (*Patrick Eagar*)

Brian a letter expressing his regrets and stressing his non-complicity: 'To me cricket has lost the best tactical captain I have known. I can only hope that I put into practice some of the ideas I have learned from watching you.'

Then there was the youthful member of the Yorkshire Academy XI who, twenty-three years later, found adjusting to life under his gruff but kindly sixty-three-year-old captain something of a culture shock: 'Cor, he doesn't half swear a lot.'

Beyond the Pennines, a lad from Cheshire conveyed his gratitude. 'He always tried to instil in me a feeling that I should never be overawed,' recalled Botham, one of two prodigies Brian (who also happened to be godfather to his wife, the much put-upon Kath) nurtured at Somerset; the other was Viv Richards, the only cricketer of the final quarter of the twentieth century to outdo Botham for self-assurance. So far as Botham was concerned Brian was 'chiefly responsible for turning Somerset from a social side into a successful one'.

'He saw things very much in black and white, and if his motto was not kill or be killed, it was certainly about imposing your will upon an opponent ... He taught [me] the only way to succeed at the highest level is to have total belief that you are better than anyone else on the field. If he had stayed around longer than [he] did ... when I was poised on the line separating right from wrong, there would have been someone close to me with the guts to stand up and say: "Don't be such an idiot".'

Ah, but did anyone apart from Illingworth have the guts to stand up to Dennis Brian Close and tell *him* not to be such an idiot? More to the point, did anyone ever advise him that the only way to succeed at the highest level – in England at least – is to realise that being better than anyone else on the field is, in itself, insufficient.

'THE LAST HOUR and forty minutes, in which Warwickshire had to score 142 to win and failed by nine runs, led to allegations of delaying tactics against Surrey and to the eventual censuring of their captain, Stewart. Surrey bowled only 24 overs, and, in the last fifteen minutes, during which they left the field to the umpires and the batsmen during a shower, sent down only two overs.'

Of the sixty-nine words above, sixty-five are not fictitious. So we can all imagine the extent of the 'censuring'. A bout of tut-tutting in the popular prints and a slap on the wrist at worst. Substitute 'Yorkshire' and 'Close' for 'Surrey' and 'Stewart' and you have the *Wisden* view of the Warwickshire–Yorkshire match at Edgbaston in 1967. It cost the national team the services of its most intuitive and dynamic leader of the post-war era.

We could, at this juncture, go into all manner of musty nooks and skeleton-crammed crannies. Brian is certainly willing to do just that, as he did at some length in his autobiography, *I Don't Bruise Easily*. (Quite possibly the most fitting title ever conceived for that dishonoured genre – 'that was the publisher's idea; I wanted to call it *I Took The Blows* after Sinatra's line in 'My Way'. I bruise like anyone else but I just get on with it.' It alluded both to his penchant for fielding suicidally close to the bat and sustaining any number of horrifying blows, as well as the myriad of strictly metaphorical sticks and stones he has had to withstand. Its contents were described with memorable bitchiness by one of his arch-foes, E.W. Swanton of the *Daily Telegraph*, as 'the longest whinge in history'.) He will tell you that *Wisden* made no mention whatsoever of the fact that the entire Warwickshire innings was conducted in drizzle without his emitting so much as a boo in protest. Or that the 'shower' was closer to a downpour. Or that when it came he had to nip to the loo. Or that his bowlers flouted regulations by drying the ball on the way back to their marks, rather than doing so under the eye of the umpires (the rule had been brought in to dissuade seam tamperers). To *save* time. Or that Gary Sobers told him that his infamous series-gifting declaration at Port-of-Spain the following March was provoked by the dilatory over-rate authorised by Brian's replacement, Colin Cowdrey.

We could also delve into the brouhaha reported in *The People* (chief cricket correspondent F.S. Trueman) under the headline, 'Brian Close Sensation – He Attacked Man In Crowd'. Brian, who had heard a Warwickshire member insult him as he left the field at lunch on the second day and duly sought out the culprit, will assure you he did nothing of the sort. He will tell you that he has a letter in his possession, from one Doug Nicholls of 87 Lichfield Road, Walsall Wood, Staffs, confirming that he merely clamped a hand on his shoulder, asked him if he was responsible for the offending outburst and, upon the denial, apologised immediately. But to delve any further would be to dignify.

Brian was dragged before the Lord's beaks on the eve of the final Test against Pakistan, hitching a lift after breaking down en route (not an uncommon occurrence; he has always treated his cars with much the same judiciousness as he selects his words; as a national selector, happily, he would choose players with greater care). Nor was he especially chuffed when he beheld the jury: two of its four members had recently been upset by his weakness for frankness – 'We'd had odd words, arguments.' He was held responsible for his side's 'delaying tactics' and 'severely censured'.

'I was flabbergasted. They hadn't a case. If Brian Sellers, the Yorkshire chairman, hadn't intervened, I'd have gone straight to The Oval and told 'em to shove the captaincy. We were fighting for our honour at Edgbaston but they'd taken away my only weapon in those situations. Brian said it was typical of the southerners. "They're having a go at us," he said. "Go to The Oval, captain that bloody side and win." So I did. At the end of the match, Doug Insole, the chairman of selectors, came up to me and said: "Well done, you've done a great job, we chose to take you to the West Indies as captain this winter but MCC overruled us." I think it was the first time anything like that had ever happened.'

Had he apologised, had he tugged the old forelock (not that he had too many locks left to tug by this stage, fore or aft), he might have saved his job. But Brian never got on his knees for anybody, not even Vivienne, his rock-cum-redeemer. Besides, why apologise for something you would do all over again without the slightest compunction? As for Sellers's 'typical southerners' comment, scepticism/paranoia of that ilk was, and remains, far from unfounded. That, though, is only part of the conspiracy theory. Brian was a maverick. And we all know how English sport treats its mavericks.

THE SUB-PLOT WAS anything but insignificant. Panic was mounting – and not before time – at the game's precarious hold on the public. At the outset of the 1967 season, the 'brighter cricket' mantra was being chanted with almost hysterical zeal. Then Boycott spent the entire first day of the opening Test cobbling together 106 against a spin-loaded Indian attack on a sun-kissed Headingley featherbed. The next day he racked up another 140 in barely half the time but it was much too much, much too late; he paid with his place, sacrificed on the altar of image, highest Test score forever tainted. Not an eyelid would have batted, of course, had the opposition caps been green and baggy.

Not that the concern wasn't eminently valid. Addressing the annual Forty Club dinner, Leslie Deakins, the Warwickshire secretary, revealed that gates for county matches since the post-war boom had dwindled from two and a half million to 500,000 – an 80 per cent loss. 'We must face the fact that we are providing a spectacle the public does *not* want,' he urged. 'At the same time we must acknowledge that we know what the public *does* want – they have told us through the medium of the Gillette Cup games.' The forty-over Sunday League was still two years away. For now, for most pros, the Christian Sabbath was still a day of rest.

It still seemed precisely that on 2 July when Lord's got around to staging championship play on a Sunday. Facing Hampshire's slowly-gotten gains of 421 for seven declared, the tenants expended more than seven hours averting the follow-on – then batted on. Whereupon Arthur Fowler, the Middlesex secretary, put his foot in it. Asked why his captain had failed to declare at 272 for seven, he replied: 'Middlesex were not prepared to throw away wickets for the sake of two points.' Or, heaven forfend, the punters.

The reference to the two points highlighted one of the more obvious causes. The previous winter, one or two purportedly bright sparks resolved that one sound method of encouraging 'brighter cricket' would be to award eight points for an outright win (down from ten) and four for a first-innings lead (up from two). As a consequence, noted *Wisden* with barely-concealed incredulity, it was possible to obtain as many points from two draws as from a victory, the upshot 'more deadly dull cricket'. The use of the word 'deadly' in those perennially understated pages should on no account be underestimated.

Even so, to string Brian up after his bowlers had delivered 'only' twenty-four overs in a hundred minutes – a rate of roughly 15 an hour, the 1998 Test minimum – inferred a separate agenda. Brian cannot be shaken from the view that it was strictly personal. Nor, one suspects, should he. While the impression of a man who feels he has been repeatedly spat on from a vast height is hard to avoid, the sequence of events suggests his grievances have substance.

THE ENGLISH ARE nothing if not pigeonhole-fanciers, steeped in that fine art of sculpting first impressions into some unchallenged truth. Brian was doubly cursed. In a land dismissive and fearful of youth, it was bad enough that he should have become, at eighteen years and 149 days, his country's youngest-ever Test player; worse still that his speed and footwork on the left flank had earned him England Schools caps at soccer and a professional contract at Leeds United at seventeen. 'As a teenager I was a better footballer than cricketer,' he avers. 'Then I had me thigh smashed up by Newcastle's Ted Robeldo. I went to Arsenal, after missing the entire 1950–51 season owing to National Service, but the injuries kept coming and I didn't last long.' No less injurious was his maiden Ashes tour in 1950–51, for which No. 22185787 Signalman Close was permitted to take a break from his duties in deepest, darkest Catterick.

'It was still fun and games then. My father had been a very good League player and I'd played for our village first XI, Rawdon, when I was eleven, but I was still a kid with only one season of first-class cricket behind me. I wanted to belt the cover off every ball, take a wicket with every ball. The thought part had never occurred. I needed help, I needed discipline, I needed playing hell with. The only person who talked to me about the game on the whole trip to Australia was the great old Yorkshire and England fast bowler Bill Bowes – and he was a pressman. I suppose I was out of my depth. I was naïve.'

Detachment begat isolation when he tore a tendon making a century in Canberra. Playing in the Melbourne Test 'with my leg literally dangling by the end', he made nought and one and was *hors de combat* for the next few weeks. By the time the bulk of the party left the mainland for the Tasmanian leg of the trek he was virtually *persona non grata*. 'They thought I was swinging the lead. Nobody was talking to me.' Denis Compton, captaining the team in the absence of Freddie Brown, ordered him to fulfil twelfth man duties on the day he was due to see a specialist. Gilbert Parkhouse got him off the hook but when Brian gave the doctor's note to his skipper, Compton ripped it up.

'He was livid. "I don't give a fig what the doctor says," he said, "you're playing in the next match." So he put me in at three. "Christ, Gilbert," I said to Parkhouse, who was due in at four, "get your pads on – I haven't had a bat in me hand for three weeks." I was overheard to say – by John Warr, I think – that I wasn't going to bloody try. Me, not try?'

On his return to Renmark he was hauled before Brown. 'What's all this I hear about you not trying,' said the skipper. Brian explained about the misunderstanding and was given a stern lecture on the professional's duty to play with a broken leg if so instructed. 'Then the leg went at Geelong and I was carried off. They laid me on the table: I was in shock. I was still lying there when they came off at tea. They all had a curse at me. That was the end of the tour for me: I didn't play again. Then I went to play golf at the Royal Melbourne with some friends during the final Test; there was no point in going to the ground – nobody was talking to me. Don't forget, I didn't drink or smoke. By the time we got back we'd won the Test but I got another bollocking. Why wasn't I there? I didn't dare say why. I was an outcast, a social outcast.'

'It'd be interesting to know the truth about Close,' ponders David Sheppard, another of that winter's virgin tourists. 'One day he came on as drinks waiter and he had to put his foot on somebody's hand, didn't he? People were always having a go at him because of his clumsiness. They were amazed he'd got his Higher School Certificate because he didn't seem to be a very intelligent young man. I think he was very naïve. He was certainly very kind to me, listening to my problems when he was having a terrible time. Wonderful, natural cricketer. In 1949 he'd done the Double [1000 runs and 100 wickets in a season] at a younger age than anybody had ever done, and without trying. Didn't know how difficult the game was. He had a very bad tour, then he was out of it for ages, but then something happened to make him this very gritty, tough competitor. Somewhere, somehow, something very good happened to him.'

Growing up was what happened. Unfortunately, memories of the nineteen-year-old Brian hardened into myth-based fact. One can all too readily picture the contents of that dusty file they pulled out at Lord's on the day of his 'trial' sixteen years later: 'Gifted boy but headstrong. Bit of a shirker. Not best liked. Needs putting in place. Not one of us. To be discouraged whenever possible.' Never again did the selectors entrust him with a senior overseas assignment.

Fast forward to 1967 and a not unfamiliar tune. 'They got rid of me then because I didn't conform. The MCC committee were all ex-amateur captains, Oxbridge. I took the HSC [Higher Schools Certificate] in 1948, at seventeen, a year early. My headmaster at grammar school wanted me to go to Cambridge and study maths – though I wanted to do medicine – but all of the university places then were going to those who'd had their education interrupted by the war. So I signed pro with Leeds United, then Yorkshire. I had more brains in my little finger than Cowdrey and all the rest of them put together.

'I grew up after the '50–51 tour: only one person was going to help me and that was myself. I became a good player. They brought me back in 1955 for the last Test against South Africa, who'd just levelled the series two–two, to open against Heine and Adcock, a real nasty pair. I top-scored in the first innings, hung around against the new ball in the second, and we won. Went to Pakistan with the 'A' team and scored as many runs as anyone, then smashed my knee up in a car accident during the Yorkshire–Australians match at Bradford – didn't play until later in the season and lost my chance of making the Test team. You could say I was a misfit.

'I had two Tests against the West Indies in 1957 and didn't let them down, then one in 1959 against India where I took four wickets for 30-odd, held four catches, scored 30-something runs and they dropped me until 1961. Came back at Old Trafford and John Langridge gives me out lbw for 30-odd when I cracked the ball on to me pads; then I get caught sweeping Richie [Benaud] when nobody knows whether we're going for victory or not.'

Behind that succinct and pithy summation lies one of the precious few instances in the Sixties of a five-day match justifying its duration. On the final afternoon, England, chasing 256 with the series level and the urn on the line, sped to 150 for one on the back of one of 'Lord' Ted Dexter's most imperious sallies, then collapsed when the Australian captain decided to bowl his leg-breaks round the wicket and into the rough outside the left-hander's (i.e. Brian's) off stump – primarily in an effort to *save* the match. Brian caught the majority of the flak, roasted in the media for getting out to a rash shot. 'It had a 60–40 chance of success, of picking up some runs,' insists this inveterate if luckless gambler. 'I thought we were still trying to win.' No matter that the Aussies' last pair had added 98 to turn a cakewalk into a race against the clock; no matter that the England captain had been bowled round his legs for a duck. Why look elsewhere for a scapegoat when Closey's around, doing something daft?

Ditched for the Oval Test, shunned throughout 1962 and again for that winter's Ashes tour, he returned to confront the West Indies, playing his one and only full five-Test series, albeit only because the presence of Wes Hall and

Charlie Griffith had placed the emphasis on courage. Intriguingly enough, his only post-1967 Test appearances came against the 1976 West Indians, whose arsenal was even more relentless and vicious, as the unhelmeted forty-five-year-old opener discovered during one outrageous evening duel with Michael Holding and Wayne Daniel amid the Old Trafford gloom; he was abruptly dispensed with – he contends – not for his safety, as professed in some quarters, but a) because he was only brought in in the first place to shield Bob Woolmer, a younger man for whom the selectors had longer-term plans, and b) because it had by then become blindingly obvious that he was the best alternative to Tony Greig, the then struggling captain.

Never were Brian's limitless reserves of gung-ho in starker evidence than in that unforgettable Lord's Test of June 1963. Compiling his Test-best of 70, he charged Hall and Griffith as if they were lobbing beach balls as opposed to grenades, striding down the pitch as they thundered in, quite content to allow the ball to beat a tattoo on his torso. Nobody intimidated Closey. He was still dumped.

Thirty Tests passed before the next recall. Once again, the Windies were in town. This time, having led Yorkshire to the championship in 1963, his first summer at the helm, and all but ensured another, the precursor to a hat-trick of pennants, Brian was drafted in as skipper. Nevertheless, as the third coin-flipper tossed into the fray against the Great Garfield and his rampant crew, he detected an ulterior motive. It was, after all, the final Test of a dead rubber. 'The press were hankering after change. I'm sure they only put me in there because they were sure I'd go the same way as Cowdrey and Mike Smith. That way they could say, "There you are" and go back to the Oxbridge boys.'

An innings win scuppered that; twelve months and five victorious Tests later he was the toast of Albion. It would have been six wins, he insists, had the corpulent Colin Milburn – who for all his crowd-pleasing biffing was a liability to his own bowlers away from his perch at short leg – not spilt a critical catch at Lord's off Hanif Mohammed while stationed in the deep. Admittedly, the opposition could have been more taxing, but still: six wins and a draw in seven Tests was a ratio no English captain had ever achieved.

All of which makes for an appropriate moment to pause and analyse how Brian had given the selectors no option but to turn to him. In his own words.

'A captain has to be a giver, and I always put the team before myself. Captaining England was the easiest job on earth when I did it because I had top players. I just had to handle them, tell 'em what we were trying to do. As a captain, of any team, you're out there to ensure everyone gets a fair opportunity. If somebody doesn't he gets downhearted and that's a weak link. And if you look at the history of cricket the best captains have been all-rounders.'

Worrell, Benaud, Miller, Illingworth, Imran and Close? More than sufficient to make a presentable case.

'We didn't always see eye to eye at Yorkshire but I didn't mind conversations. I didn't mind arguments, because you know damn well that when people are emotional they speak their mind. And if you know what's in a person's mind you're halfway to getting them to play well. I think I made more people play better than anyone had any right to expect.

'Cricket is like chess except the pieces are human beings. And human beings are often irrational. I tried to forewarn youngsters about what they could expect out there, just as I'd learned from listening to Maurice Leyland and Bill Bowes. I was brought up to believe that there was only one reason to go on a field – to try to win. Nothing else was acceptable.'

Did he draw a line? 'Oh yes. You wouldn't do anything that was dishonourable. I never sledged. I only talked to an opponent on the field if he spoke to me first. What do you mean? Cheat? I never did that.'

No, merely that, had you led England in 1932–33, say, would you have acted as Jardine did? 'No. I don't think I believe in that sort of thing. I believe in bowling at the stumps. Then placing a field according to the ability of the batsman. I knew what people's weaknesses and capabilities were. If I saw someone lunge forward I knew he didn't know where his off stump was, so every couple of overs I'd suggest a good-length ball two foot wide of off. Those balls are harder to play than a straight, good-length one. You don't necessarily have to bowl a good ball to take a wicket.'

According to many a respected judge, the game in England relinquished much of its adventure and chivalry with the extinction of the amateur captain. Brian – surprise surprise – is not among them. 'I'd say there were two reasonable ones I played under: Norman Yardley at Yorkshire and Donald Carr for the 'A' tour to Pakistan in 1955–56. They put the game first but I don't think they studied the effects of the way people think. Well, I'd learned that through my failures and successes. I knew what went on in people's minds, and I was able to anticipate them. I'd go to [wicketkeeper] Jimmy Binks and ask him how a batsman was playing and within a few minutes I could work out how to get him out.'

BRIAN'S SUSPICIONS WERE aroused not long after Milburn's muff, stoking his belief that he remained an outcast. As Exhibit A, he cites a tip-off from Crawford White, respected cricket correspondent of the *Daily Express*. 'Crawford rang me up and said: "Brian, for Christ's sake, watch your step, because they're after you. They want you out and their own man in. They think you've put the team together and they don't like it." Their man being

Cowdrey – yes sir, no sir, three bags full, sir.' They being the selectors and the MCC, under whose flag England touring teams still flew.

'And yes, it *was* my team. Wouldn't have had it any other way. I insisted on bringing Illy back when none of the selectors wanted him; I didn't get anybody I didn't want – except Milburn.' At the press conference to announce Cowdrey's reinstatement, Doug Insole, doyen of the parried question, made an uncharacteristic lapse. Bowing to pressure from the assembled hacks, he confessed: yes, had Brian not been hauled over the coals after the so-called Edgbaston Affair, he would have been the selectors' choice to lead in the Caribbean. 'It was the classic press that were after me, the MCC press – the *Telegraph*, *The Times* and the *Observer*. They spoke up for the establishment.'

Brian's luck was out again in another respect. That very winter, the MCC would finally cede control of English cricket, giving way to a Test and County Cricket Board representing, and run by, the first-class counties. As international results went from sorrowful to pitiful, the self-interest of the constituents would prove a hindrance, so this may not have been a wholly unmitigated boon, but at least idealism started taking a back seat to realism. The decision to veto the selectors' reappointment of Mike Gatting twenty-two summers later, taken for kindred reasons by Ossie Wheatley (Cambridge University, Warwickshire, Glamorgan and MCC), demonstrated that the new boss – to invoke The Who once more – was pretty much the same as the old boss. Brian's, nonetheless, was the last head to topple into the tumbril of the *ancien régime*.

LAUGHTER PERMEATES THE cool afternoon as he relates these misfortunes. He can see the ludicrousness, appreciate the inevitability. Those furry eyebrows soar more than they knot. Being sacked by Yorkshire was an ambush worthy of the VietCong: he never saw that one coming, not for a second. 'I drove away [from Headingley] with my mind still in a whirl. I wanted to cry. As I drove along Kirkstall Road my vision misted up so much I had to stop. And then I was sick, there at the side of the road.' Fury followed.

I Don't Bruise Easily (Brian's favoured title seems ever more apposite at this juncture) traces the events of 25 November 1970 in a chapter entitled The Worst Day Of My Life. Again, an abridged version will suffice. Again, why dignify? In 1970, Yorkshire finished fourth in the championship, a rise of nine. Lancashire, however, emerged one rung higher, only the fourth time Red Rose had topped White in twenty seasons. Worse, the Old Traffordians lifted the Gillette Cup for the first time and retained the John Player League title they had annexed in the competition's inaugural season; the White Rose was deflowered in the first round of the former and withered to fifteenth in the latter. A pattern had been set, had they but known it, for the remainder of the millennium.

'The most disastrous [season] in the history of the club,' attested the Yorkshire CCC annual report. Losses amounted to £8000. Their bitterest rivals banked £5000 in prize money alone, but that was just the icing. On August 30, by way of rubbing it in, an estimated 33,000 were shoehorned into Old Trafford and saw Red Rose trounce White by seven wickets to secure the forty-over crown; not since 1948 had Lancashire closed their gates during a match.

A scapegoat was needed. Why not a thirty-nine-year-old with a dodgy shoulder and an even dodgier grasp of the theory and practice of obedience? There was an almighty outcry, and one of Yorkshire's fabled Action Groups forced 'Crackerjack' Sellers to resign as chairman of the cricket committee, but the damage had long been done. Misguided, handled with the utmost insensitivity and botched from first to last, the whole affair could scarcely have reflected more poorly on Brian's employers had they accused him of not caring. Which is, effectively, exactly what they had done.

The way Brian interpreted it, there could only have been three reasons for jettisoning him:

1) He wasn't fit. Plausible but unlikely. He had missed half-a-dozen championship fixtures after injuring a shoulder in May, and sent down only twenty-one first-class overs all summer, yet he still achieved a higher batting average than specialists such as Phil Sharpe and Doug Padgett, neither of whom were discarded.

2) He didn't 'bring on' youngsters such as off-spinner Geoff Cope. Implausible. As a man who claims to have an uncanny memory for detail (and none at all for figures), he can rubbish that in five seconds flat.

3) He loathed the limited-over game (or 'instant rubbish' as he sneeringly termed it). Plausible *and* possible. While recognising that its popularity was the only means of keeping the superior format commercially viable, he regarded it as the root of all evil. And still does.

This distaste, however, did not mean he didn't know how to play the wretched game, or win at it. Never mind that he had piloted the side to the sixty-over pot in 1965, the Gillette Cup's third season (when he 'inspired or frightened Boycott into playing the innings of his life', as Jackie Hampshire put it in *Family Argument – My 20 Years in Yorkshire Cricket*). Never mind that he had repeated the feat of the previous year. Never mind that he would be recalled to lead his country to victory in the 1972 Prudential Trophy against Australia, the first official limited-overs international series anywhere. Never mind that he planted the seeds of Somerset's belated rise to prominence as the power of the county one-day circuit, cajoling them to within one run of the 1976 John Player title, which would have been the first honour in their history. 'It might be argued,' wrote Eric Hill, that titan of the Taunton pressbox, 'that the overall achievements of an unfancied side suggested that his fiercely demanded requirements might have provoked some players into performances beyond their normal capabilities.'

Jackie Hampshire believes the situation was exacerbated by Yorkshire's refusal in 1968, the year of Trueman's acrimonious farewell, to give Illingworth the financial security he felt was his due, prompting him to accept an offer to lead Leicestershire. The following spring, Cowdrey's achilles tendon snapped; up stepped Illingworth, now established as the Test team's number one offie. Within two years he was being fêted as the second England skipper to retrieve the Ashes in Australia since the *Titanic* went down.

'If Illingworth had stayed with Yorkshire,' surmised Hampshire, 'Close's supreme and oft-broadcast contempt for the one-day competitions in general, and the John Player League in particular, would have been under some restraint. Illy would quite simply have told him to "bloody well shut up" when Close was about to embark on yet another tirade against the damage that limited-overs cricket was doing to the first-class game. The trouble with Close was that he cared so deeply for county and Test cricket that it represented his whole world and anything that was likely to have an adverse effect upon it was total anathema to him.'

Nor is Brian about to issue a retraction. 'Cricket is a very emotional game. The art is out there in the field – how do you get this bloke out? It's the fielding side that asks the questions. But over the last twenty-odd years we've reversed that because of all this bloody limited-overs cricket. We have too much of it here; we need to get the balance right as they do overseas in their domestic cricket.

'At first-class level, the players dictate the game. In limited-overs, the game dictates to the players. How on earth can you learn how to captain a Test side that way? Bowlers aren't thinking right. When a youngster comes in to the side, rather than being able to express himself, he's thinking, "God, I must save runs or I'll be taken off". It's totally negative. The bowlers aren't thinking, "shall I try an outswinger this time?". They're thinking: "I wonder what the batsman's going to do. Back away? Reverse sweep?" I spoke to Illy the other day. He's never seen such badly-directed bowling since he started in the game. All concentrated outside off. Bowl six balls outside off and everyone applauds!' The laughter is as hearty as it is empty.

'I spoke to Ted Dexter about all that when he became England supremo at the end of the Eighties. I used a racing analogy because I know he likes his horses. If you took a racehorse, could be the best in the world, and you put it over a two-mile hurdle one day, a six-furlong sprint the next, a three-mile chase the next, then a mile-and-a-half middle-distance run the next, it'll wonder whether it's stood on its arse or its elbow.'

WHATEVER THE WHYS and wherefores of the Yorkshire verdict, one fact is indisputable. Brian, a man out of time and glad of it, was wounded to the very quick. As somebody whose commitment could be faulted only in its foolhardiness, who was willing to shed blood for the cause, to laugh at the very notion of self-preservation, who loved not wisely but too ruddy well, he deserved better. 'The Yorkshire sacking hurt more than losing the England job,' he avows. 'I'd devoted me life to Yorkshire.'

So why did he continue to do so after his West Country sabbatical? Why did he consent to join the committee, and then become chairman of the cricket committee? Why didn't he tell them to stuff their gestures of conciliation? More pertinently, having resigned from the cricket committee a couple of years back, following the installation as chairman of Tony Vann, a man for whose qualifications he held little bar contempt, why was he at Headingley today, revelling in Craig White's 50, cursing every Surrey breakthrough, not to mention those fast-dissipating plans to shift the club's HQ to a spanking-new 35,000-capacity stadium in Wakefield complete with retractable roof? And why did did he scold me, however gently, for not honouring his blessed palace with a tie and jacket?

'Oh,' he chuckled, seemingly taken aback that such a question could ever have been posed, 'I don't bloody well hold grudges.'

Chapter 4:
The Coach's Tale

'Don has been the most wasted
talent in English cricket'

Mike Gatting, 1997

IT ALL DEPENDS ON ONE'S interpretation of the word 'coach'. In the States they'd probably have immortalised him with a chocolate bar. Crunchy DB, perhaps – jagged outer layer, soft and gooey in the middle. After all, they did name the land's most sought-after sporting bauble after Vince Lombardi, the autocratic 'coach' who piloted gridiron's Green Bay Packers to a mere two Superbowls then had the prize itself christened in his memory. During his three decades as 'coach' to Middlesex, Don 'DB' Bennett presided over the most glittering reign in modern county history: seven championships (Schweppes and Britannic), four NatWest/Gillettes, two Benson and Hedges Cups and a Sunday League. At the very least, amid an era of unparalleled humiliation for the national team, one might have expected his expertise to have been called upon by his country. Guess again.

W

e always seem to go for the big names, don't we?' bemoaned an admittedly biased Mike Gatting in the summer of 1997, just as the soulmate who counts him among his two greatest discoveries prepared to vacate the wings after forty-seven years on the Lord's credits. 'We don't stop to look for people who have shown they can do the job day in and day out. Don hasn't pushed or promoted himself and he has been wasted. He is the best coach I've known by some distance. He gives you confidence as a player, and if something isn't working his remedy is always simple. And he knows what he's looking at when it comes to judging players.'

Ay, and there, quite possibly, lies the nub. Even Don will admit that he is far from the world's foremost technician, that he is first and foremost a scout with a perceptive and precious eye. Mind you, there was a time when he was adamant that Gatting's prospects were inferior to those of my one-time Stanmore colts captain Andy Needham, a useful off-spinner, steady bat and infinitely shapelier chappie who even now blushes at such misjudged flattery. Then again, perfection is so insufferably boring.

The fact was, Don's direct influence over onfield matters was minimal. For twenty-seven of his twenty-nine summers as coach, HMS Middlesex sailed serenely along under the auspices of just two skippers, the two mighty Mikes: Brearley and Gatting. Brears and Gatt ruled the roost; Don got on with hatching the eggs. He freely admits he was driven by his own shortcomings. 'Maybe I didn't quite have the temperament to succeed as a player in the way I'd have liked. That's why I'm so keen for others not to make the same mistakes.'

Don had been exposed to the harsher realities at a tender age. In 1940, when he was six, his father whisked the family from Yorkshire to Ashford, Middlesex, to take up a post at a borstal that had been converted into a prison for wartime purposes. The young DB was not shielded from the nuances of the job. A quarter of a century later, he was inveigled into playing a game of football against a prison team because he knew the terrain; he was 'clobbered' by a warden. Never again did the former Arsenal winger kick a ball in anger.

Given such a background it should come as scant surprise to learn that Don became a stickler for dress codes and discipline (though not so much that he objected to boys being boys). Just like Gatting, who finished his first team talk after succeeding the more laid-back Brearley with '... and don't forget there'll be no jeans on match days or away trips'. Don kept the kids in line, fired and hired, prodded and steadied. He also knew his place. 'I have always thought there could only be one boss of a cricket team,' he declares, smiling that chummy, toothsome smile. 'And that's the captain, so I always knew where I stood. I saw myself as a sweeper. Coming round the back, picking up the bits and pieces.'

As a shirehorse, Don's record was more than fair-to-middling: a shade over 10,000 runs at 21.88 and 784 wickets for that lively seam-up at an admirable twenty-six. Yet how much more impressive might it have been but for those fourteen winters of muddied oafing? Having twice come close to selection for England tours – to the Caribbean in 1953–54 and South Africa three years later – surely he must have wondered?

'No, never. It was much more clear-cut then. Playing both games professionally was just a way of life. The first-class season was effectively over by the end of August and Les Compton and I used to go straight to Arsenal after that. They'd send us on five and seven-mile road walks in those old army boots. Les and I would do five miles, and Arthur Milton, who'd come back from Gloucestershire, would do the seven miles because he was such a superb athlete. We used to get some cracking finishes coming up Avenell Road. There were no holidays. Well, one long holiday.'

And then there was Closey. Don reckons his fellow Tyke could well have become another double international had the green-eyed monster not reared its head. 'Good footballer. Arsenal got rid of him because he was getting too much publicity, on account of playing for England at cricket. I think the players got him moved out. He was unreal. I love him. I was in digs with him. He took me for my first game of golf. I think the world of him, but he didn't help himself either. Too honest. Quite refreshing, really.'

A RARE CLOUDLESS June morning ushers in the final day of Southgate's first first-class match since the American Civil war. At first glance everything seems precisely as it was. On the second day, the Friar Tuckish Gatting and his perky

Australian partner Justin Langer had set a county record opening stand of 372. Before the torrents came the ex-skipper had cheerily addressed the press in front of the scoreboard while the snappers snapped. My, how those silvery whiskers on his chin had glistened with delight. Staggering to the stumps like some battered frigate contending with a force-ten gale, Angus Fraser was now beheading the Essex openers, Indian summer in full swing. Don perches himself on a chair next to the candy-striped tent and enclosure reserved for members of the Middlesex committee, the insider on the outside.

'I've lived without it better than I thought,' he grins, reflecting on Saturday's deluge. 'Fortunately, if it rains now I won't have to hang around. I can go home. I still check the scores on Teletext. We've moved house and I've played some golf. I've enjoyed watching the Test matches because it's given me a chance to study techniques, of people like Atherton, which I've never really had the time or opportunity to do before.' How did it feel coming back and not being involved? 'Strange, actually. I purposely kept away early in the season because I felt that'd be the time, if I was going to feel anything, I'd feel it then.'

Success had long disguised the generation gap, but by that final season it had been positively deafening. 'The ghettoblaster goes on in the dressing room at eight-thirty,' he had told David Townsend of *The Sunday Times* shortly before hanging up his tracksuit. 'It's a relief when one of the older players manages to slip on a bit of Elton John. I'm getting too old for it all.'

Not that that had made the parting any easier. 'Obviously I've missed the boys. I came on Saturday – that was the first time since last year I'd seen Ramps [Mark Ramprakash, the other discovery to do most to puff out that ample chest]. I haven't purposely avoided him but that was the first chance I'd had to talk to him. I've been to watch the second XI kids a few times. I've always enjoyed that more really, seeing them come through. Seeing a kid, a colt, and thinking, yeah, he could be good. That buzz when you spot talent is *beautiful*, but tracing them through – that's the most exciting part of the job. Always has been.'

At that very moment, who should mosey over but titchy old Fred Titmus, the erstwhile England off-spinner and sparring partner whose reluctance to retire in 1969 left the way clear for Don to become only the fourth coach in Seaxe history. History, indeed, had repeated itself the previous winter. Scenting a hundredth first-class hundred, Gatting, Don's anointed successor, elected to carry on plundering, allowing John Buchanan, a studious, camcorder-toting Australian, to inherit the mantle. For all those impressive figures littering the Southgate scoreboard the new regime was mired in quicksand. Middlesex, who would ultimately fail to bowl Essex out on that most placid of tracks, were en route to their most woeful season for more than two decades. At Hove they would be bowled out twice in a day. Some wag said it was their heaviest drubbing since the last

Home sweet home… In his first summer of retirement, Don Bennett returns to Lord's, 'the office' for more than 40 years – July 1998 (*Graham Goldwater*)

Below left: Reeling in the years… Don Bennett and Fred Titmus walk out to open for Middlesex at Wye, 1966 (*Don Bennett Collection*) and (right) reunited at Southgate, July 1998 (*Graham Goldwater*)

Summer breeze… Don (*back row, second from left*) lines up for Middlesex in 1952 alongside John 'JT' Murray (*top right*), Jack Robertson (*bottom left*), Bill Edrich (*bottom, second from left*) and (*bottom, middle*) Denis Compton (*Don Bennett Collection*)

Winter content… Alex James (*centre*) entertains Don and Brian Close during their Arsenal days (*Don Bennett Collection*)

lousy Labour government. Fraser's restoration to national colours, Phil Tufnell's listlessness and Jamie Hewitt's elusive confidence had left the attack next to toothless. The youngsters were struggling, even Don's most recent prodigy, Owais Shah, the England Under-19 captain. Dissatisfaction was rife, notably among those more set in their ways. Rumblings were mounting.

The lofty Buchanan had guided Queensland to the first Sheffield Shield titles in their history by dint of scrupulous attention to detail and a we're-all-in-this-together philosophy embracing such defiantly non-Middlesex concepts as family barbecues. Even during their 1980 pomp, when John Emburey (Peckham Manor Secondary) and Clive Radley (King Edward Grammar, Norwich) marched out shoulder-to-shoulder with Phil Edmonds (Cranbrook School and Cambridge) and Wayne Daniel (Princess Margaret, Barbados), the Seaxes were driven by creative friction. 'There were some very strong, very different personalities in that dressing room,' deadpans Don. 'People were able to express themselves, and it could be quite explosive, but when they went out they went out *together.*'

Two hurdles had loomed ominously for Buchanan. For one thing, the county programme is that much more frenetic and all-consuming than its Aussie counterpart, affording less scope for preparation and bonding. Second, and of immeasurably more significance, Ramprakash, Gatting's successor as captain, had expected to exercise the same privileges and undemocratic control his predecessors had enjoyed. Buchanan, though, was used to being more hands-on than Don on first-team matters, more accustomed to calling shots.

Come September he would be on his bike, undermined at every turn, position all but untenable, even though this so disenchanted the supportive Fraser that it hardened his resolve to seek more progressive pastures. Still a few hundredweight short of that ton of tons, Gatting, now forty-one, retired to claim his rightful throne as director of cricket, a dynasty restored.

Don was quite content to be at one remove. Miffed when passed over for the cricket committee, he realised that this might be seen as politically tactless. How could he, in all conscience, be party to passing judgment on Buchanan? All the same, one could sense a feeling of rejection. He had proposed setting up a scouting network but that was still plonked in the in-tray. Bob Gale, long-time teammate and now chairman of the committee, a chap he had been used to conversing with on a daily basis, had not phoned 'in months'.

By the time we reconvened at Lord's in August, Gale had broken his silence. He wanted to discuss that scouting project. Results had deteriorated; the rumblings were now snarls. Public ones at that. Up in the scorers' box the phone rings. Gatt here: could somebody get him the up-to-date figures for Shah and David Nash? Don was still trying to keep a distance but you could tell he was itching. There was no pleasure whatsoever to be had from seeing friends struggle.

It was odd being back at the old palace, feeling so detached. He thinks the new Grandstand 'looks nice' but prefers to reserve a final verdict on the half-completed media centre between the Compton and Edrich Stands, already nick-named 'The Gherkin' by certain sections of the press but rechristened 'The Silly Sausage' in the aftermath of an exclusive poll conducted for *The Guardian* by a correspondent with the dubious name of Slogger.

'I remember the first day I came here on trial. It seemed a long way from Ashford. The bloke we were bowling at, Reg Routledge, who I knew, was getting hit all over the place by this six-foot-three fast bowler, so Gubby (Allen) starts getting his kit on. "'Ere," I thought, "what's this old bugger doing?" Must've been forty-seven, forty-eight. Then he said, "Boys, are you all right for another twenty minutes?" then called out "Martin, where's my net?" He had his own special net! Class player, good on the on side. Bowl one on his legs and he'd say, "Laddie, don't bowl there: I'm the best on-side player in the world".

'We bowled quite well so he asked me and this other lad back to the com-mittee room for a drink. My clothes weren't that smart. Anyway, we're watching the game – Middlesex *v* Hampshire – when Walter Robins walks in. "Ah, Robby," said Gubby, "these are the two boys who've done so well." So Robby looks at me and says, "I see you're in your Sunday best". I walked out. I thought, "How can two great names be so different, one so nice, one so awkward?" I suppose it sums up Lord's for me.

'Middlesex don't own the ground so you have to watch your step, in the nicest way. But overall they've been bloody good. The MCC made me an hon-orary member; I was thrilled with that. But if I could change one thing I think it would be that Middlesex owned their own ground. There's a limit to what you can earn this way but there's also the question of identity. Maybe we should amalgamate with the MCC?' The grin resurfaces. He knows full well he is speak-ing of a club whose idea of enlightenment is to consider admitting women (emancipation was still a couple of months away).

Had he had any contact with the players since Southgate? 'No *real* contact,' he replies, lips pursed. 'You can't win with that, especially when things aren't going your way.' On his last visit to HQ, the sight of Shah moving carefully to a century had buoyed him no end. 'He's got all the shots but he needs to decide what ones he can and can't play. Getting better off the back foot, too. When he was a kid he never had to move off the front. They'd pitch it up and he'd smack it back.' Suddenly, he confessed to having had a hush-hush liaison with Hewitt, Fraser's heir apparent. 'He's having a bad time. Somebody asked me to have a look at him in the nets but I said I can't. I can't win if I do it here because it undermines John Buchanan. As long as I saw him somwhere else it'd be OK. So I did. He was low on confidence. He'll be all right.'

BACK TO SOUTHGATE, to jollier seasons. To 1950: Don's first spring on the groundstaff, Titmus' second. Interjecting only with the occasional nod, Fred listens as Don salutes his original coaching mentor, Alf Gover. 'There were no indoor nets at Lord's then so they used to send us to Alf's on a Sunday morning. When I was at Arsenal and my form started to deteriorate I asked Gubby whether Middlesex would send me to Gover's on Sunday afternoons. "Look," said Alf. "Don't worry about Middlesex. We know each other. You get here and I'll look after you." After that I worked with him. He was brilliant. Gave a lot of his time free to the professionals, a bit like a cricketing David Leadbetter. Arthur Wellard was there too – tremendous.

'Alf didn't pay much so he was always looking for coaches. He used to have musicians and all sorts. One day he went off for an appointment somewhere leaving Arthur to oversee the four nets. There were no bowling machines then so you had to do it all yourself, and by half-past three on a Sunday afternoon, having already trained at Highbury in the morning, I was a bit knackered. "Keep goin', keep goin'," said Arthur. "You're by far the best coach here." Right, I thought, I must be pretty good at this. Then I looked across and in the next net was a drummer, and in the next a saxophonist. That's how Alf made it pay. He cut costs to the bone. But I learnt a hell of a lot. He was very good on bowling, as you might expect, but also excellent on batting. He told you what to expect, how to look after yourself. Wonderful man. Still is, though I haven't seen him for a couple of years. Closey played golf with him; they were big mates. First professional cricketer ever to be invited to join the Golf Society, y'know. I used to coach a team of cabbies there. Bloody keen they were. One day one of them said to me, "This cricket and football thing's a bit precarious: get something behind you – do the Knowledge." So I qualified as a cabbie. I bet I'm the only one ever to park in Gubby Allen's parking space.'

Don remembers the day Alf concluded that a hands-off approach was much the most sensible means of prolonging his autumnal years. On the eve of the MCC's 1960 Caribbean venture, Peter May turned up at Wandsworth for a net and promptly drove an offering from Alf straight back with that customary withering force. Alf grabbed the net and pulled it towards him to parry the ball. It still struck him a juddering blow on the heel, persuading him once and for all that physical well-being was now paramount. 'I was scared when I bowled to May that day,' recalls Don. 'There wasn't a lot of room to manoeuvre.'

'I've been very lucky in my coaches. I had Alex James at Highbury, Alf and Gubby, who was always there in the background, great on technique. Alec Bedser and Jim Laker were great too, even when you played against them. "Play a bit straight you silly bugger," they'd say. "What do you want to play through there for?" Just after I gave up my job in personnel management to take the

Middlesex job I had a long talk with the golf coach John Jacobs. Peter Parfitt had a golf day for his benefit and John talked to me for two hours afterwards. Told me I had to give the players a picture of what they were doing at the moment, and another picture of what you want them to do. He talked about the shape of a drive, which is the same in bowling, the way in which the ball leaves the hand. I used a *hell* of a lot of what he told me.

'The sad thing for me was that I played in an era when England, for once, could call on any number of top-class fast bowlers – Trueman, Statham, Tyson, Moss, Loader – yet we never employed any of them as coaches. A hell of a lot of expertise went missing. I also wonder whether the uncovered wickets we used to trounce everyone on gave us a false idea of our own ability.'

Fred smiles wistfully as Don recalls the Terrible Twins. 'It was never the same after Compton and Edrich packed up. You used to sit there fascinated by Compo. He didn't like watching the game, didn't turn up very early for practice, very rarely had a net. If he wasn't batting he'd be getting ready for lunch. Always brought some smart gear, always the touring blazer. He used to put it on in front of the big mirrors just inside the dressing-room door: "Look all right do I, boys?" Then, if it was a Saturday and there was a big crowd in, he'd pop out to the balcony and look out – I can see him doing it now – and wave. And twenty women would wave back. They'd fall over themselves. Like Titmus, Compo never watched the cricket. He had that magical quality, like Arnold Palmer. He could walk through a room and make everyone feel as if they knew him personally. He didn't drink much then. In fact, I didn't realise how little he did drink. Edrich took me behind the bar one Saturday night after Compo had bought a few rounds and there were fifteen drinks that had barely been touched: all Compo's. He watched it very carefully, especially if he had a bit of crumpet.

'But what a player. I batted quite a bit with him, especially early on when I went in at six. He wasn't very good on a Monday morning; Saturdays in front of a big crowd was another matter of course. Against Sussex one time I'd made 20-odd and he was on 99; there was no pressure on but I thought I'd better show I was keen so I started really backing up. After four balls of this he says, "do me a favour, don't worry about the single – with a big crowd like this I'll hit it for four". Next ball or the one after he hit it for four. Then he said, "I think Bill [Edrich] would like a bowl tonight so we've got about twenty minutes; I don't want you to have a slog but you won't see much of the bowling." Boomp, boomp, boomp, boomp – got 40 in no time. I had two balls, I think.

'People always talk of him as a terrible runner between the wickets but he wasn't that bad because he was never the one that got run out. He only did me once, in the first game I played with him, and that was my fault. He had tennis shoes on and it was his first game after the knee operation, so I thought, if I send him back I'll finish him off. So I ran past him and had a dive.'

Until the watershed summer of 1963, Titmus was billed on the scorecard as 'Titmus F.J.' and Don as 'Bennett D.'. Were they relieved when the class-ridden distinction between amateurs and professionals was abolished? 'I'm not sure it's ended now,' smirks Don. 'Look at some of the appointments on the ECB. Still all Oxbridge. I think they might eventually bring Durham University graduates into the fold. It's still there.

'It was tough as a young kid when we began. Quite a few fell by the wayside because they couldn't cope with the authority figures, with the forelock-tugging.' Which brings us back, not unnaturally, to Closey. 'The way he was sacked by England was a bit harsh. A lot of people would have got away with that.'

MIKE 'SMUDGER' SMITH, that slender and prolific Middlesex opener-turned-scorer, remembers Don as 'a compact, correct batsman, particularly against slow bowlers, at five-foot-ten ideally six inches too short to be a top bowler, always flat at you, so you saw the length very early'. Their paths first crossed while they were going in different directions: Smith graduating to the seconds, Don demoted.

'It was a pretty traumatic time for Don being left out after a decade, a real blow to the pride, but unlike some in that position there was no chip on the shoulder. To be perfectly blunt, the second half of his career was a bit of a disappointment but sometimes that disappointment makes a better coach or manager. He was always low-profile, even in the successful years. He obviously had a talent for recognising who could and couldn't play, but he was also a back-up, a go-between. He was always the backbone, the stability factor. He gave the club discipline, forged the link between the first and second elevens. Under his predecessor, Jack Robertson, discipline had been very lax. The club couldn't understand the yobbish behaviour of the seconds and, at times, the firsts. I think Jack was moved on because he couldn't handle us.

'Don has a terrific gift for making people wary of him. It's part of the armoury. He was great at putting people in their place, not a bloke you'd want to get the wrong side of. The first-team players still approach him with trepidation. He prepared the youngsters for life in what was, after all, a highly individual first team. He had that loner air about him that marks the disciplinarian. I'd known him for thirty years by the time I started scoring. When we were playing away I'd come down for breakfast half an hour before everyone else, same as him, but we didn't always share the same table.'

Brearley made some predictably acute observations, dividing Don and his breed into 'undercoaches and overcoaches'. 'There are often different and opposite ways of falling short of perfection. Cricket coaches may overcoach or they may undercoach. The former is more often the most damaging. Down the net they go after every ball, blowing batsmen's brains with the variety and perceptiveness of their advice. Overcoaches impress, but do not teach. Undercoaches damage, of course, by neglect. But many *apparent* undercoaches are in fact doing an important part of their job; they watch and they wait. They allow growth naturally and individually, building on particular strengths, rather than on an abstract idea of excellence. If he errs in either direction, Don falls into the latter category, but the more players know him the more they respect him.'

Mike Roseberry, the teenage prodigy who fulfilled at least some of his abundant promise at Lord's before returning to his native Durham as captain in 1995, will gladly testify to that. 'People talk about Don as being just a talent-spotter but he was a great coach. During my first couple of years I didn't know quite how to take him. He seemed so quiet, so nice, then he'd really give me hell. I suppose I'd picked up a few bad habits staying on at school, getting to 20 then smashing it to mid-on, but I learned a great deal from him. He wasn't worried about the mental side, purely technique. A few years later, after I'd left Middlesex, I was going through a bad trot as captain and batsman so I had a word with Don about coming to the Lord's nets that winter. To Durham's credit they agreed; I was going to and from London twice a week, had eight or nine sessions, facing Fraser, Hewitt, Johnson, all the senior bowlers. Don organised it. He was a huge help. And he did it all on Middlesex's time.'

Don's own favourite treatise sprang from the pen of his ever-dapper old mucker John 'JT' Murray, Test stumper and centurian. 'That's the best article I've ever read on coaching,' he enthuses, producing a copy of his own testimonial brochure and flicking to an item headed 'You don't have to be a good player to be a good coach'. The author, he insists, 'has more vision than any cricketer I've ever known'. He and JT, he hastens to point out, had joined Middlesex on the same day, and got pie-eyed together the night JT's daughter was born. 'In theory a coach's job is quite straightforward, to make people better players – to utilise their ability to the full,' mused JT. 'A coach cannot make a player, he cannot possibly put in ability which isn't there, but if he says the wrong things he can easily spoil it and leave a player at sixes and sevens. There are many factors to coaching, some requiring a real understanding of the game, others not.'

Whichever way you look at it, Don, whether as talent-spotter, groomer, honer, sergeant-major or bottle-washer-in-chief, did comfortably more than his bit to make his club the silverware factory it was from 1976 to 1993. Fortune, he repeatedly stresses, was seldom a stranger. 'The good players tended to come in batches. We were pretty lucky but you've got to be flexible. Go out into the Minor Counties: there's a lot of good players out there. Wilf Slack came from Bucks. Sheer chance. After I retired from playing I went to work in High Wycombe and got to know a few people at Slough. One day Gouldy (Ian Gould) wanted a bit of match practice so he went to play for Slough and asked me to come along. It was a glorious day but there was only one other person watching besides me. I went over and asked him if he knew any useful players at High Wycombe and he recommended somebody named Slack. I was a man short for the Under-25s that Thursday so I rang this bloke and asked him if he had Slack's number. He was twenty at the time, fairly advanced. I gave him a game and that was it. I signed him soon after.'

The dominance of those Under-25 sides, states Don with nary a smidgin of boastfulness, tilled the soil from whence the flowers sprung. He also suspects it kept him in a job. 'Things didn't go very well for the first couple of years. I needed a bit of luck, a bit of know-how. Then I was offered a one-year contract and I thought, "I know I'm struggling here". By sheer chance they'd just started the Warwick Pool Under-25 competition, so I thought, "I'd better make a dart for this". We had some good players and we won it the first two years: Middlesex had won nothing since ... when?' Since 1949.

'Brearley cottoned on very quickly. "How do you see it?" he asked. "Well," I said, "I think we can win this, but I need Edmonds, Selvey, Butcher, Barlow and all the other boys who are eligible from the first team." "You got 'em," he said. And that changed everything.'

The credit for Simon Hughes' blooming as a writer may not be unconnected to the fact that, during his summers as first or second change behind the Grace Gates, it was not uncommon for him to be the only non-international in the side. He had to find another means of excelling. Here, indubitably, was a team to tremble the sturdiest knees. There was the Caribbean-bred pace and craft of Wayne Daniel, Neil Williams and Norman Cowans, complemented in the covers by Roland Butcher, another member of the so-called 'Jackson Five', and Graham Barlow, the only contemporary English fielders to give Derek Randall a run for his money. Runs came solidly – Brearley, Clive Radley, Larry Gomes, Slack – as well as extravagantly – Gatting, Barlow, Butcher, John Carr. Then there was the judicious choice of imports, from chunky Desmond Haynes of Barbados, junior half of the game's most consistent opening pair, to towering Vintcent van der Bijl of Natal, the finest bowler never to win a cap. The masterstroke, though, lay in uniting the chalk and cheese of Philippe Henri Edmonds and John Ernest Emburey. For a decade and more Middlesex could call on the most incisive English spin duo since Lock and Laker. Together they harvested the best part of 2500 county victims. Accidents, once again, will happen.

'They're *so* different,' marvels Don. 'Embers was the complete professional, brilliant. Phil was a great lad but hard work. I used to say to him, "Look, you bowl some world-beating balls but you don't put too many out of six in the right place". He didn't really take any notice. He and Brearley didn't get on, but only the other day I saw him and he said to me, "I was a prat". I said, "Yeah, in a word". He asked me how many Tests I reckoned that had cost him. Might have been fifteen, twenty. I told him he was a bloody idiot because he couldn't win.'

Both came to Middlesex after having paths blocked elsewhere, Emburey by Pat Pocock at Surrey, Edmonds by Derek Underwood at Kent. 'Arthur Mac [McIntyre, the then Oval coach] told me he had a bloody good offie but couldn't afford to keep him. They were down to fifteen full-time pros by then, as we were. "Right," I thought, "I'll have a look at him." I had to go through the official channels, bring him in for a trial. After Embers had bowled two or three overs I said, "Right, that'll do". His face went glum. "Oh," he said, "I thought I'd get a bit more of a chance than that." I told him I was going to take him on. "Oh," he said. Took him to Kent to play for the seconds and Bob Woolmer was batting at three for them so I thought I'd better not bring him on until Woolmer was out. But he got a hundred so I had to bring him on – and he did Woolmer in his first over.

'But Titmus was still around, and even when Embers did get a chance it didn't work out, so Fred came back towards the end of the 1976 season and helped win the championship. A few weeks later Embers rang me up and said he'd been here for five years, didn't seem to be getting anywhere and was thinking about accepting another offer. By sheer chance I'd been to a meeting at Lord's that afternoon and Fred, who'd just retired, said he was going to coach at Surrey. It wasn't official, but ... So I asked Embers to give it a week, and that if I couldn't work something out I'd help him go. I knew there'd be a committee meeting that week. The following Monday Embers came in and said, "You crafty old sod".

'Phil was up at Cambridge. Typical Phil: pain in the arse even then. Majid Khan was captaining Cambridge and he told me I had to get him for Middlesex, that he'd talk to him for us, that he'd like to come to London, lot of talent. "Thinks he's a fast bowler," he said, "but he's really a spinner." I didn't know until two or three years ago that Glamorgan, whom Majid was also playing for, were also trying to get Phil then. And there's Majid trying to help me out! I don't know what it is. Luck? Good contacts? I'd played against Majid a few times and we'd got on, but ... If it wasn't pure luck it was bloody near.

'Edmonds could spin it like a top but he was never consistent. He got the yips once. "He's yours," said Brearley. He came with the seconds to play against Essex: said he wanted to captain, open the bowling and the batting. His first ball went over Keith Pont's head, the next went along the ground, the next was a pearler that pitched leg and hit off. He never liked training. Nor did Embers. He'd bowl for an hour, an hour and a half: that was his way of getting fit. And, unusually for a senior player, he bowled properly. He'd bowl at anyone. That's how Slackie [Wilf Slack] learned how to play spin. Gatt, too. Phil Tufnell's the same now, always giving it everything.'

Guiding light... Don with some youthful pupils and Harry Sharp (*far right*), Middlesex's scorer during the glory years (*Don Bennett Collection*)

Godfather and sons... Don looks on as Angus Fraser, Phil Tufnell, Mike Roseberry and Mark Ramprakash salute captain Mike Gatting at Hove after Middlesex had won the 1990 county championship (*Don Bennett Collection*)

Above left: Refreshing the memories…
Peter West with the author, and (*right*)
tout seul, Worcester, 1998 (*Graham
Goldwater*)

Right: Auntie's boy… Peter with BBC
commentary colleagues Jim 'EW' Swanton
(*left*) and Brian Johnston atop the Oval
gantry when England won back the Ashes
in 1953 after a 19-year drought. The
cameraman is Bill Wright, who went on to
produce *Mastermind*

Thunder road... Peter provides shelter from the storm at Edgbaston as Richie Benaud does his implacable, impartial best to assess England's chances of winning the first Test against Australia in 1975: they lost by an innings (*Patrick Eagar*)

Sunny afternoon... Peter elicits some modest reflections from Geoff Boycott after the opener had scored his 100th first-class hundred before his adoring fellow Yorkshiremen during the fourth Ashes Test at Headingley, 1977 (*Patrick Eagar*)

Expert view... Peter mans the cans as John Edrich, Tom Graveney, Jim Laker and Benaud monitor England's progress against the West Indies, Headingley 1980 (*Patrick Eagar*)

Last waltz... Peter interviews the England captain Mike Gatting and his Australian counterpart Allan Border during the fourth Test at Melbourne, 1986 – England's win secured them the Ashes for the last time this millennium (*Patrick Eagar*)

Below: Puff and the magic dragon... Peter with trademark pipe, Tony Greig and the Channel 9 Weather Watch machine, Melbourne 1986 (*Patrick Eagar*)

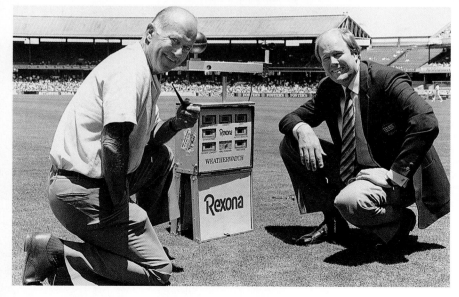

And so to Gatt and Ramps. Both tarried in making a wider impact: Gatting required more than fifty innings to record his first Test ton; Ramprakash had mustered just one in nearly as many attempts. The former eventually flourished: can the latter? 'I think he will. I hope so. It would be tragic if it doesn't happen for him. But he's got to *make* it happen. They've shoved him up and down the order, which hasn't helped. Now he's at six and each time the tail has been blown away in next to no time. I first saw him when he was eleven or twelve and even then he always seemed to be determined to prove something. And yes, it might well have had something to do with having a mixed-race background. The first time I saw Ramps smile at the crease was when he reached that hundred in Barbados during the winter. With Gatt you always had the impression he enjoyed it.'

AMID ALL THE popping corks came the fizzle of mortality. On 15 January 1989, a few weeks after his thirty-third birthday, Wilf Slack, devout Christian and arguably the gentlest man ever to bat for a living, suffered heart failure at the crease during a private tour of Gambia; he never regained consciousness. Professional sportsfolk are not exactly renowned for outward displays of affection – something to do with maintaining that macho competitive edge, no doubt – but here was a man whose generosity of spirit and self-effacing *bonhomie* melted all resistance. When Phil Tufnell won the *Daily Telegraph* Sportsman of the Month award for his match-winning performance in the final Test of the 1997 Ashes series, the artful dodger donated the cheque to the Wilf Slack Trust, a charity set up to improve cricketing facilities for youngsters of Caribbean extraction in London as well as their counterparts on the islands themselves. In death as in life.

Slacky was one of Don's beloved 'boys', the shy St Vincentian he'd been tipped off about at Slough. He'd fought his corner when the committee wanted shot of him. 'You must be mad,' he had harrumphed. 'Slacky's the best player of fast bowling in the country.' Slacky stayed and went on to open for England. It was his record opening partnership with Barlow that Gatting and Langer would eclipse at Southgate. When he collapsed during the 1986–87 Ashes tour the management were quick to flick the matter beneath the nearest shag-pile, but the following spring he confessed to an eager young hound from the *London Daily News* that he had in fact been perilously close to death. Not only that, his condition was such that another attack could recur at any time. Don, needless to add, had long been privy to this.

'Slacky's death was horrible, even though we knew it was likely to happen. He'd dropped down in the nets once, and keeled over facing the first ball of a match against Leicestershire. Facing Jon Agnew: let the ball go past and slumped to the ground. Something to do with the valves of his heart, something more common among Africans and West Indians. They passed him fit and he got through another season then went across to Gambia. One of the saddest things about his death was that it happened in January, when we were all scattered over the globe ...' Words briefly fail him.

'What a great bloke, but he knew the risk. "Listen," he used to say, "if I can't play cricket I might as well be dead anyway." The pair of them had a fair amount in common.

Chapter 5:
The Commentator's Tale

'The BBC did not apologise to viewers who were deprived of seeing half of Botham's century on Saturday at Old Trafford because somebody in his wisdom decided precedence should be taken by a horserace from Newbury and the Midland Bank Horse Trials.'

Richard Ingrams, 1981

THE BALL CRASHED into the right side of his face, fractionally below the eye. The redness of the projectile led me to anticipate the worst. Happily, such fears were unfounded: since when do they make red tennis balls? The seventy-eight-year-old victim, nonetheless, was decidedly shaken. Gathering himself, cheek throbbing, he asked his assailants, a group of Gloucestershire players, if they wouldn't mind moving away from the pavilion and practising somewhere where the odds against endangering life and limb were rather longer. Quietly. Politely. Reasonably.

Unflappable and unforced, brimming with authority and rectitude, the voice, albeit a tad agitated, remained every inch as measured, every drip as honeyed. It still reeked of apples snaffled from the head's orchard, of a cloistered, mothballed world where Britannia rules fields as well as waves. Where the score is forever 2–0 or 230 for two, Johnny Foreigner is getting a dashed good kicking and the BBC cameras are on hand to capture every single self-affirming shot. Civility and pipe to the fore, Peter West and his vaguely superior but affable Home Counties tenor were the very personification of that world.

If you were in possession of a television or radio in Britain between 1946 and 1986 you would have found it hellishly difficult to avoid 'Westie'. Granted, he wrote as well, reporting many a Five Nations for *The Times* and an Ashes tour for the *Daily Telegraph*, the latter an unexpected bonus after he retired from Portland Place: until then, his dual commitments had prevented him from covering a major overseas expedition in either rugby or cricket, in *any* capacity. It was the younger mediums, though, that made his name.

If he wasn't presenting *Come Dancing* he was commentating on the All Blacks and their unique brand of tangos and polkas. If he wasn't interviewing Percy Fender or Miss World he was hosting panel games like *Why* or *Guess My Story*. If he wasn't bantering with Richie Benaud or Dan Maskell he was playing straight man to Terry-Thomas (Benaud, indeed, reflects on his formative years in the booth with Peter and Brian Johnston as a 'priceless experience'). If he wasn't promoting the razor-sharp qualities of Gillette, West Nally, his sports promotions company, was brokering the sponsorship deal that paved the way for the Benson and Hedges Cup. Freelance though he may have been ('Be independent' urged his manager), he was an integral part of Lord Reith's Beeb, the Beeb of Richard Dimbleby, Raymond Baxter and Alvar Lidell; the Beeb of Harry Carpenter and Henry Longhurst, of John Snagge and John Arlott; a Beeb that valued sport as its most reliable means of plugging into a perceived British consciousness, of reaching 'the nation'. On 15 October 1998, that era finally expired, puttering and sputtering to the last.

Tradition, a wise man once warranted, is the illusion of permanence. Which is why two far-from unconnected events in the space of twenty-four hours that month can safely be described as shattering. From Lord's came the announcement that a two-day meeting between the First-Class Forum (comprising representatives of the eighteen first-class counties and the MCC) and executives from the England and Wales Cricket Board had yielded accord on an unimagined scale. Appealing to pockets as much as hearts or minds, Lord MacLaurin, the ECB chairman, together with his trusted cronies, had drawn up a five-year plan for the professional game involving a substantial increase in internationals and a two-division county championship. Both were accepted in principle.

A year earlier, when the latter was put up as a panacea for a domestic game not only lacking the edge of true competitiveness but keener to promote quantity than quality, cocks were snooked, the count twelve votes to seven. The board's argument was logical enough: the best way to retain eighteen professional clubs, institutions whose very existence depends on the income flow generated by the national team, and simultaneously improve the fortunes of that team – thereby wooing a generation alienated by failure – would be to introduce promotion and relegation and/or end-of-season playoffs. The roots of the resistance were no less logical: a tiered structure would breed domination by the haves (i.e. the Test ground clubs) and extinction for the have-nots. That the fearful had been persuaded to reconsider was partly down to some shrewd manoeuvring; the haves, it was proposed, should accept a reduced share of the pot and the surplus redistributed at all levels. It was also attributable to a belated acceptance of reality, an acknowledgement that Something Must Be Done.

The following morning I received a call from a mate in the Channel 4 press office. The new TV contract had been signed and, would you Adam an' Eve it, they'd secured the rights to virtually every home Test for the next four seasons. The ECB, it seemed, had been much taken with a sexy, snazzy, ultra-modern presentation that promised to bridge racial and generational divides. Flabbers, even so, were well and truly gasted. When Channel 4 and the ECB released the official announcement at 4 p.m., gobs were smacked from Land's End to John O'Groats. Channel 4's chief executive did make the grave error of proclaiming that his team would portray Test matches as 'thrilling and exciting', but it was difficult to avoid the conclusion that the Beeb had got its just deserts. Had it not been for those enterprising vibes from Lord's, moreover, it is highly unlikely that Channel 4 would have tabled that conclusive £100 million-plus joint bid with Sky. In an age where 99.9 per cent of the population experience their favoured sporting tipples from sofa or bar, this was regarded, with a modicum of justification, as a matter of the utmost national importance.

The decision by a House of Commons Select Committee to 'de-list' home Tests – i.e. remove them from the list of sporting events deemed so intrinsic to the fabric of our lives that they must be shown on terrestrial television for The Greater Good – had alerted us to the possibility that that ambitious Mr Murdoch might muscle in on the Lord's showpieces. But no Beeb at all? Unthinkable. No Richie to wish us G'Mornin'? Inconceivable (in the event, much to the nation's gratitude, the ageless maestro would sign for Channel 4). No pauses for *Neighbours*? Unconscionable. Leader writers harrumphed; irate letters flooded into the *Telegraph*. In other quarters, Whitehall included, derision was heaped on Broadcasting House: for penny-pinching, for complacency, for arrogance. Losing the FA Cup and Formula One to ITV and the Ryder Cup to Sky was bad enough, but *this*? Was this the end of civilisation as we knew it?

Peter wrote to me shortly afterwards. He was saddened, of course. 'Richie can name his terms. In spite of all the absurd talk about livening up the presentation, I believe the new channel, apart from jazzy trailing *à la* Sky, will avoid national uproar if they reveal the game with the same authority and dignity as the Beeb and Sky.'

AS HE NURSED that swollen cheek that misty moisty Worcester morning, the man who anchored Auntie's Test coverage for fifteen summers was only too delighted to extol the virtues of the new order. From our left came the inimitable squeak of Dickie Bird, now almost halfway through his farewell season. Barnsley's newest pensioner was chatting animatedly to a couple of spectators with that familiar fusion of schoolboy angst and showman-like self-parody, enjoying a flap while he still could. He was perfectly aware that the rain had ceased and the light was playable, but he couldn't very well start the game because the England selectors *still* hadn't confirmed whether they wanted Graeme Hick and Jack Russell to dash to London for the Lord's Test. Nor would finding replacements for this game be a piece of cake. Oy vey!

Rather than sending him into an indignant froth, as some might envisage, the commentary team at avowedly non-terrestrial Sky Sports has captured Peter's imagination. 'I rate Tony Lewis very highly for his work after succeeding me, but Mark Nicholas is doing a terrific job too. I always felt that if he'd made a few more runs he'd have made a very good England captain. Talks a bit much but he's very good, very intelligent, nice personality, good interviewer. Paul Allott's interviewing is good too. I wrote him a note recently, congratulating him on his interview with Mike Atherton after Mike had given up the England captaincy, which was superb, one of the best I've ever heard. He passed the note on to his producer, who replied to me. I recently wrote letters to two of the producers with whom I'd worked at the BBC and never got a reply.

'I raised a point about them not showing us how many runs a particular batsman has got. It's quite possible to be out in the garden – I call myself an unpaid gardener these days – and pop back just before tea to see how it's going, then wait twenty minutes to find out how many each batsman has made. They put the total in the top right-hand corner but they don't show the ground scoreboard anymore, do they? It's improved a bit since but it's not perfect. Even the commentators don't do it. In my view, it should be a golden rule on TV: if the scores are not shown by your camera director at the end of an over, you should give it. But that's virtually the only complaint I've got.'

He even speaks highly of R.G.D. Willis, for all that the erstwhile England captain and Bob Dylan *aficionado* had been responsible for some of his most least pleasant moments as a broadcaster. It all began at Trent Bridge in 1980, some thirty-four not-so far-flung summers after Peter had been dispatched to Taunton by the Exchange Telegraph and instructed to ask Wally Hammond to supply him with Gloucestershire's XI for the next match: in both instances the words 'fuck' and 'off' figured prominently.

There he was on Thomas Parr's old patch, lurking at the pavilion gate, mike in hand, waiting to interview the England fast bowler after a spirited but luckless day against the West Indies. Bob Willis, who at that juncture regarded the media with about as much affection as a cobra lavishes upon a mongoose, recommended that Peter stuff his interview where the sun steadfastly refuses to shine. At Headingley a year later, after Willis had destroyed the Australians and pulled off the most treasured English sporting victory since '66 And All That, Peter approached Mike Brearley, the victorious captain, seeking permission to speak to the hero on behalf of the great unwashed. 'Bob's in the bath,' he was informed. 'You can ask him yourself.' Peter picks up the tale:

'I knocked on the door of the England dressing-room and was bidden to enter. Stretched out in a bath absurdly small for his elongated figure lay the fast bowler, contemplating his navel. "Bob," I said. "Well bowled. Tremendous. Will you come and talk to me on the tube?" He gave me another of those searching looks. "What," he replied, "about Lord's last year?" [the pair had met in a hospitality tent a few weeks after their Nottingham contretemps; when Peter took Willis to task for being "rude", the latter turned tail, he recalls, "in high dudgeon"] "Surely we can forget that," I went on. "It's been a marvellous day for English cricket." Bob thought about it again. "All right," he said. "I'll be with you in five minutes." Duly appearing in front of the camera, he knocked the wind out of my sails and, to judge from the mail I subsequently received, astounded many viewers by launching himself into a condemnation of the media. We were still "live" on the air … "Bob," I said, "you've just won a Test match in the most remarkable circumstances. Can't we stick to a happier topic?"

This, I am glad to recall, diverted him to a much more acceptable theme.'

The animosity soon passed. 'When Bob joined the BBC experts panel we got on very well. I have to hand it to him: he may not have the most attractive voice in the world but he's really worked at it, become very professional. And I think he's bloody good. Doesn't mind what he says, does he? He's blunt. The whole Sky team is bloody good – and all the better for not having Boyks.'

This last laughing reference is, of course, to the controversial Sir Geoffrey of Boycottshire. 'It's people not very close to the game who like him. What he says is very good and very interesting but when you've heard the same thing three times in four minutes it becomes a bit wearing, doesn't it?'

SHORTLY AFTER THE Headingley fiasco, an article in *The Times* observed that Willis, 'having punctuated the ultimate triumph by delivering a coruscating general denunciation to a squirming Peter West … withdrew from journalists altogether.' This distrust, shared by Brearley and Botham, who these days also work with the hand they once bit, had two distinct sources: the provocative excesses of tabloid papers embroiled in a circulation war, and the growing realisation that the nation's cricketers could no longer be depended upon for succour.

By the onset of the Eighties the revolution had come, seen and conquered. Media magnate Kerry Packer had secured a ten-year deal to cover and promote Australian cricket on his Channel Nine network, the leading players whose services he had requisitioned from all over the globe to force the issue were back in the fold, and the progressions initiated by the polo-preferring Sydneysider were beginning to generate profits for all. Out in the middle, moreover, the power now lay with the New World, with Australia, West Indies and Pakistan, as it would thereafter. Headingley turned out to be a mirage, a magical, fleeting flirtation with a past life.

How different things were for Peter's maiden Test on the goggle box. Old Trafford '52 and a swarthy, swaggering young Yorkshireman by the name of Frederick Sewards Trueman reduces the hapless Indians to five for three, then 17 for five, then 58 all out: eight for 31 told. (Intriguingly enough, the only eight-wicket haul for an out-and-out fast bowler for England since then was Willis's eight for 43 at Leeds twenty-nine summers later.) The previous October, manufacturers announced plans to produce 250,000 TV sets in 1952 and predicted that the number in British homes would double from the current 344,000 within two years. With transmitters now ensconced in the Midlands and Manchester as well as London, and Scotland due, four in five of the population, it was promised, would soon have access. This at a time when, according to the 1951 census, one household in three was bathless.

Wild west heroes (1)… Somerset pose for the *paparazzi* at Leicester, 1951. *Left to right, back row:* Roy Smith, Les Angel, Maurice Tremlett, Reg Trump (scorer), Eric Hill, Jim Redman, Ellis Robinson. *Left to right, front row:* John Harris, Johnny Lawrence, Harold Gimblett, S. S. Rogers, Bertie Buse, Harold Stephenson. Gimblett, the 'Tormented Genius', was the subject of David Foot's acclaimed biography (*David Foot Collection*)

Wild west heroes (2)… (*from left*) Tony Brown, David Foot, David English, Ian Botham and Vic Marks field questions from the floor (*David Foot Collection*)

Above left: A dose of Andrews…David Foot at the Weston-super-Mare Centenary match, 1975, with Bill Andrews, the Somerset stalwart to whose fabled autobiography 'The Hand That Bowled Bradman' he lent his liquid literary touch (*David Foot Collection*) and (*right*) in reflective mode at Cheltenham, July 1998 (*Graham Goldwater*)

The King And I… David listens intently to Viv Richards, Weston-super-Mare, 1983. While working for the BBC he was the first to broadcast Richards' feats for Somerset back to the Caribbean (*David Foot Collection*)

All you need to know about Peter's suitability for his new role is contained in a BBC photo of himself, Brian Johnston and E.W. Swanton on the TV gantry at The Oval in 1953. The first things you notice – apart, that is, from the lavishly Brylcreemed cameraman and his buck teeth – are Peter's tastefully greased hair and pristine parting. Compare that to EW and his Etonian Latin master's crop. Immaculately besuited and groomed, Queen's English as crinkle-free as the knot in that sober tie, restrained of emotion and sparing of gesture, Peter embodied what was expected.

Back to '52. 'There was a gale blowing down the pitch and Fred coming downwind. My god, the Indian lads were a bit apprehensive. I didn't speak to him afterwards because it was all black-and-white and three cameras, with no recording and no zoom lens. Space was cramped and the summariser would do his job in the rain. And we weren't doing interviews.' I inform him of the deliciously serendipitous circumstances surrounding my own initiation: England *v* West Indies, Oval '66, when Tom Graveney sculpted 165 of the most exquisite runs imaginable, instantly transforming sceptic into zealot. The eyes light up. 'Ah, Thomas. I was hoping he'd be here for lunch today. He must've gone straight to Lord's. I always believed that when rain fell while we were on the air together, and we had to keep going, the Graveney–West duo might enjoy going on forever, even though in the end they might have bored the pants off most of those looking in.'

During his Kentish boyhood Peter had harboured sporting aspirations of his own, playing cricket and rugby to a more than tidy standard at Cranbrook School (as a distinguished old boy maintaining strong ties with his *alma mater*, he would later coax star-studded MCC XIs to grace its square). When a back condition put a sudden full stop to active involvement he was 'bitterly disappointed'. This sounds suspiciously like a rather massive understatement.

'I'd have gone on playing club cricket, maybe made minor county level, although I was temperamentally unsuited to making large scores. I had the shots but not the patience. They always say batting is eighty per cent concentration; I don't think I had that. But rugby I did have hopes for, probably wild hopes. Never mind, I've been more than adequately compensated. If I had carried on playing cricket I wouldn't have been able to stay in touch with the first-class game the way I did. I've had a great deal of fun, probably been the envy of a lot of my friends.'

A Home Counties accent was deemed something of an advantage back then, of course. 'I suppose it was. I suppose anything else just wasn't considered proper. Hah, hah, hah. I used to get letters calling me a southern softie, a swank. Hah, hah, hah. I don't think anyone objected to the pipe, mind. I haven't smoked for four years, you know. After forty years the doctors said I'd better give it up. My wife said it was the only reason she married me.'

Like Graveney, who himself fell from favour at the Beeb, Peter was found guilty of that most nefarious of modern journalistic crimes: being insufficiently critical. He holds his hands up more than willingly. 'I think I was *sympatico*. Cricket's a bloody difficult game to play. Nobody drops a catch on purpose. Everyone has his black moments but I don't see the need in public to castigate players. I think one should take a civilised approach. They're all trying their best. But it's becoming a harder world in that respect. Mind you, I think the English, particularly the media, have always tended to build 'em up and knock 'em down.'

In his introduction to *Flannelled Fool and Muddied Oaf*, Peter lists some of the multifarious unflattering adjectives deployed by the press to characterise him: 'bland, boring, childish, cliché-ridden, cloying, colourless, deferential, fatuous, futile, gauche, impolite, ingratiating, nauseating, officious ...' (and we haven't even got as far as the Ps). How did he respond to these darts?

'You learn to take it. Obviously when I started I was sensitive but the longer I went on the more confident I got, and the more I realised that in showbusiness, particularly TV, you're not going to please all the people all the time. The first commentary I did on radio was in 1947 – Alan Melville's South Africans – and BBC facilities ran to a tiny little cubicle just above the visitors' dressing-room. These great men – Melville, Viljoen, Rowan – could almost hear every word I was saying. I was very nervous. I wondered whether they would approve of what I was saying. Now, in old age, I have come to the conclusion that I'll say what I think and if they don't like it that's just too bad. I was always prepared to say if somebody had played a dreadful shot, but I'd say something like, "His captain won't be too pleased about that". But I've always felt that criticism should be constructive. That's fair.

'The media are more aware of television now, have finally come round to realise that it means a great deal to the public at large. That's how most people see their sport. I think there's always been an undercurrent ... envy isn't the word – but suspicion. I wouldn't say it's the money. Some cricket reporters who are friends of mine have made a lot more money than I did. I made more out of one commercial, a voice-over that took me about an hour to record, than I did in the whole of a cricket season. Ridiculous. There *has* been envy: television sport, any kind of television sport, started to get in first, before the press. Reporters were quite right to feel aggrieved about their comparative lack of access, but you wouldn't have expected me, representing TV, not to make sure I got the first interview.'

MORE, ARGUABLY, THAN any other sport, cricket has reaped the fruits of televisual technology. But for the coverage and patronage of the small screen, the game in Britain would be bankrupt. Most of the freshly-fangled contraptions, indeed, came courtesy of Packer. Initially reviled by the authorities, Channel Nine gave birth to multicoloured togs, white balls, black sightscreens and night games, the very elements that created a new, younger, less deferential audience, reinventing and reviving a form of entertainment wholly at odds with a society somewhat longer on choice and disposable income than either time or concentration.

Reverse angles and instant replays, slo-mos and super-slo-mos, SpinVision and miscroscopic close-ups – all have enhanced the viewing process while gradually making umpires redundant (but more of that anon). Some developments irk. Did Peter approve, for instance, of the decision to start showing action exclusively from behind the bowler's arm?

'I wasn't happy at the time but I've come round to accepting it, totally, even if I would like to know from time to time which end they're bowling from. Nick Hunter – who ran the BBC's Test coverage for so many years and was the best producer I ever worked with because he understood and loved the game – always said to me, "You're out of date Westie, you'll get used to it". He was so right. Having more cameras is good, although I do think they overdo the replays. Three out of five are probably revealing and the other two tell you absolutely nothing. But, to be fair, the director hasn't got time to rehearse shots. He just has to punch them in, make sure he hasn't missed anything. It's all very slick.'

Given all these visual aids and distractions, did the art of commentary change during his career? 'No. The basic essentials still haven't. I think it's much more difficult to commentate on television than radio. Radio is your own thing: you're the eyes and ears of the listener, so it suits you if you like to be the chap who's telling the whole story. It's more satisfying, whereas on TV you're part of a great big machine really – cameramen, lighting crew, sound crew and God knows what else.

'You've also got the eternal problem of how much to say, because whatever you decide to do you're not going to please everybody. I always remember the head of Outside Broadcasts on my first job at the BBC issuing an edict which is absolutely timeless: the art of TV commentary is to know when to say nothing. It's true, isn't it? I think we've all talked too much over the years – and I suppose this is a mild criticism of Sky, whose coverage is so good. Because they've got the commercials coming in between overs they tend to talk too much; they know they're not going to get a chance otherwise.'

That said, Peter's respect for some of the more, shall we say, turbo-charged motormouths remains undimmed. That these include Tony Greig, one of Packer's major henchmen, is an irony not lost on a man who greeted World Series Cricket (aka Kerry Packer's Flying Circus) with all the distaste one might expect of someone who had always seemed to be joined to the establishment hip. 'I was very upset when Tony, who was then captain of England after all, joined Packer. I resigned my Sussex membership. But I later worked with him on telly and I came to respect him as a good pro.'

Much as the milkshake-addicted Packer's express priority was to wrest TV rights from the Antipodean Auntie, the Australian Broadcasting Corporation, did Peter not agree that the enterprise ultimately made the lot of the professional cricketer more commensurate with his standing in the community, however inadvertently? The laughter is entirely self-directed.

'Looking back on it I think I've been totally inconsistent. I got to know Tony pretty well when he came to work with the BBC on a Test series in England and I respect him enormously for his professionalism. We've been good friends since. I'm sure he feels a bit hard done-by all the criticism that forced him to flee the country. In retrospect he was right and I'm sorry I took so stubborn a view. He certainly did a lot for his fellow professionals. Richie [Benaud] never talked about his involvement but he was right as well, wasn't he? And whatever the, quote, "establishment" unquote thought of him then, they respect him now. Remarkable man is our Richie. Best of the TV commentators.'

Did he ever see the Ice Man waver? 'No. Never. Not a bad name for him either. He never flaps about anything. Ice cool. Doesn't suffer fools gladly. Great wry sense of humour, tremendous knowledge of the game. He was one of the great captains, of course. Always willing to analyse, astonishingly alert. Extraordinarily quick to pick up on some small detail that nobody else would spot. A master of, when in doubt, say nothing. His silence is often quite golden because you can imagine what he's thinking. If he disagrees with an umpire's decision he'll just say, "we-ell". Silence for ten seconds and we all know what he thinks.'

The nomination for bespoke radio commentator is no less predictable or just. 'John Arlott. Master, absolute master. Not suited very well to TV but an absolute master. He painted pictures. Had a wonderful vocabulary.' He and Arlott were among the last of the BBC's specialist – as opposed to 'expert' – commentators.

'The ex-players are all over TV now, aren't they? That's one reason I had to be grateful that I was the last survivor of the club-player era. Bryan Cowgill, then head of Outside Broadcasts, decided to make me the presenter and that kept me going for another fifteen years. Otherwise I was out on me ear. He sacked Brian Johnston, sent him back to radio, which was his true *métier*.

'My strongest recollection is not commentating at The Oval in 1953 when Denis Compton swept that four to bring back the Ashes. We all did our half-hour on, half-hour off. I wasn't due on, Johnston was. Blast him!' The tone is strictly affectionate. 'Very lovely man, didn't have an enemy in the world. It didn't really matter. I was so thrilled. We hadn't won the Ashes since '32–33. It was a big moment – as it will be when we win them back.' The certainty of the 'when' defies contradiction.

Mike Denness, who had the distinct misfortune to run up against Dennis Lillee and Jeff Thomson in 1974–75, did not enjoy the most illustrious of reigns as captain of England. Nor was he left in any doubt as to his popularity when a letter plopped on to his mat addressed to 'Denness, cricketer'. 'If this ever finds you,' it read, 'the Post Office have a higher opinion of you than I have.' In *Flannelled Fool and Muddied Oaf*, Peter cites this as a prize example of the sort of abuse all those in the public eye are obliged to take on the chin. He speaks from experience.

In some respects it was only right and proper that the man from the Beeb should have broken the news that Brian Close had been turfed out as England captain, scooping the blushing boys in print. In a televised discussion aired on *Sportsview*, Peter was pitted against that eloquent Yorkshire terrier Michael Parkinson, who, neither unnaturally nor unreasonably, defended his fellow Tyke to the hilt, branding the affair a crass attempt to put a northerner in his place and a southerner in his stead. 'I said that I had always respected Close as a brave and resourceful cricketer, as a forceful captain, but it would be a sorry thing if what he had done at Edgbaston was now to be regarded as an acceptable part of the game. I suggested that if he had apologised for it, if he had admitted that he had allowed his zeal to outrun his judgment, he might well have remained as England's captain.'

A day or two later Peter hiked to Harrogate to report the vital championship match between Yorkshire and Gloucestershire for *The Times* – and promptly stopped play. 'The booing and catcalling began as soon as I had turned inside the gates and made my way in front of the stand. Halfway through the day's first over, Gloucestershire's Tony Brown stopped in the middle of his run-up and all the players looked to see what the commotion was about. I had a quick decision to make: beat a prudent retreat or keep going, the pavilion in my sights, and sweat it out. I rejected the spineless course. The pavilion seemed a long way off, and the booing went on until I got there. I found temporary refuge with Close and his men. "Bowled Parky for nowt," the captain said with the broadest of grins and not the slightest sign of malice.' For the next three days he was taunted and abused by the less forgiving.

Passions were still aflame at Headingley the following summer. Arriving for the start of the fourth Test against Australia, Peter was sought out by a superintendent and informed that he would need – and get – full police protection. An anonymous missive had been dispatched from Goole. 'We beg to inform you,' it began, punctuation declining rapidly, 'that if Peter West comes to Leeds for the

Test match, there is going to be trouble we are going to bash him we shall get him one way or the other it is no hoax he is hated all over Yorkshire and we intend to get at him and it will be as well if he does not come.'

Too ungrammatical not to warrant precaution, the pragmatic response was to have Peter escorted throughout the entire five days by a boy in blue. 'I survived unscathed,' wrote the escortee, who could hardly have been blamed for suddenly acquiring an ailing grandmother in Wagga Wagga. 'My official escort, a keen cricketer, rather enjoyed the assignment.' And they call that Aussie the Ice Man? Nutters United 0 Stiff Upper Lips 1.

Chapter 6:
The Writer's Tale

If you want me, you can find me
Left of centre, off of the strip
In the outskirts, on the fringes
In the corners, out of the grip

Suzanne Vega, *Left of Centre*

'IF ANYBODY had told me I was one day destined to make a reputation as a writer on cricket I should have felt hurt.' Neville Cardus was responsible for that haughty disclaimer. It is difficult, nay impossible, to imagine David Foot subscribing to those sentiments. It's not that he hasn't dabbled in worthier professional pursuits. He covered the trial of the last woman to be hanged in Bristol, made a documentary for the BBC about the perils of glue-sniffing, and claims to have been the first radio reporter to broadcast a female sterilisation ('I knew the consultant gynaecologist – he smuggled me in as a visiting doctor to watch the operation'). As I write, he is planning to revive his long-standing ambition, to pen an anti-war play, as seen through the eyes of the mother of a dead soldier.

Here, to be sure, is a man of many gifts and aspirations, some fulfilled, others not: gardener and pianist, dramatist and critic, sketch writer and stand-up comic. 'Sit-down comic would be more accurate,' he suggests in that disarming 'aw shucks' manner of his. At the village hall in East Coker, scene of the blue-remembered hills of his Somerset upbringing, he would don pyjamas, perch on a chair and dunk his feet in a bucket of water. Which is pretty much all the proof you could ask for when he tells you he has 'a thing about anonymity'.

Cricket, for all that, has been his main stage, cricketers his dearest performers. More importantly, and utterly unlike Cardus, his ego is as miniscule as his heart is big. In his fifty-two years as a journalist, a profession in which a penchant for *schadenfreude* can be a passport to fame, fortune and a photo byline, nobody has understood cricketers better. Nor shown them more compassion.

THE GREENSWARD'S reputation for inspiring writers to sublime if often fanciful heights is as well-won as it is exaggerated. As a provoker of prose, after all, boxing has been more rousing, baseball more symbolic of national identity. That Nick Hornby could have been spurred on by Surrey CCC rather than Arsenal FC seems impossible. Ron Shelton, the American screenwriter and film director, has created heroes and villains out of golfers and basketballers; David Storey (*This Sporting Life*, *The Changing Room*) attacked the English class system via rugby league; Alan Sillitoe's hero was a lonely cross-country runner; Martin Amis reserves his erudition for tennis. By the same token, the cricket match is the perfect vehicle for the storyteller.

Merely by dint of the time it occupies, its scope is wider than that of other sports. Throw in those imperceptible shifts in plot and that unending struggle between the me and the we, *et voilà* – a whole host of prime stitches from life's rich tapestry. Hence the inordinate tonnage of ink and paper devoted to a game followed more in spirit than flesh. Through his reporting and especially his books, David Foot, unlike most, has taken the opportunity to scrutinise what it reveals about the human condition.

Forget Cardus, Arlott and C.L.R. James. With all due respect to each of those profoundly perceptive gentlemen, nobody has proffered more warming or telling glimpses of the professional flanneled fool than the Bard of East Coker. Once, while interviewing David, my good friend Huw Richards was astonished when the interviewee described himself as 'a jobbing journalist'. Huw rang me shortly afterwards, flabbers still gasted. 'Footie – a jobbing journalist,' he chuntered. 'That's like Eric Clapton calling himself a session guitarist.' Not being quite as fervent an admirer of Ol' Slowhand, I'd prefer to compare it to Al Pacino characterising himself as a capable utterer of consonants.

On an aesthetic level alone there is more than enough to captivate readers (and turn we *bona fide* jobbing journos a lurid shade of green). The words are simple, unpretentious, unforced; instinctively sifted and sieved, never overdone or wasted. Similes deployed as sparingly as butter at a margarine convention; sub-clauses subordinated; alliteration avoided. The sentences and paragraphs, concise and precise, have the sonorous rhythmic beauty of a lyric by Cole Porter or Smokey Robinson. There are mornings when you want to recite rather than read, to share the earthy eloquence. Peter Ustinov once did a series of TV adverts for *The Guardian* in which he sat in a wicker chair reading extracts from reports by the paper's pantheon of spiffing sports writers. Unaccountably, there was nothing from David, which may or may not have had something to do with his comparative anonymity alongside the Keatings, Engels and Laceys. Yet for all that he has never covered a Test match or World Cup or Olympiad (nor really wanted to, if truth be told), the combination of Ustinov and the Bard of East Coker was a marriage made in sensory heaven.

Yet what truly sets him apart are his books ('The great joy with them is that you don't have any bastard sub-editor changing things: there's a certain indulgence'). Reasoned and resonant, they allow him to do what he does best: peeling away the layers, uncovering the humanity behind the figures, the boy beneath the helmet, the grime beyond the white. Damaged goods and clay feet are the house specialities. 'I'm not very analytical,' he insists, not fooling you for a millisecond. Underpinning it all is that unswerving fairness, that staunch refusal to build 'em up, knock 'em down and leave 'em for dead. That compassion.

The jury is still out on his contribution to the time-capsule. My mate Huw plumps for *Cricket's Unholy Trinity*, a bitter-sweet tale of the maverick breed: Charlie Parker (one of only three men to take 3000 first-class wickets yet who played for his country but once), Cecil Parkin (who pulled the plug on his own international career by daring to criticise his captain) and J.C.W. MacBryan (whose solitary Test spanned just three hours). Others swear by the masterly profiles and psychological burrowing of *Beyond Bat And Ball*, winner of the Cricket Society Literary Award. I can't decide between *Harold Gimblett – Tormented Genius Of Cricket* and *Wally Hammond – The Reasons Why*, runner-up for the William Hill Sports Book of the Year in the gravest miscarriage of literary justice since the credits were omitted from the Old Testament. Both say more about the sporting mind than all the tabloid confessions in Wapping. Inasmuch as he would ever hint at vanity, David is proudest of the Gimblett. One for the ages; one from the heart:

> *Harold Gimblett was the Somerset boy who engendered affection like no one before or since. He was a hero in the grand manner: yet the bravura never needed the flourish of the extrovert showman. He chose to leave Somerset in a quirk of unhappiness and was perhaps pining for home again in the days leading up to the taking of his life. The demons in his head caused him finally to reject his native county and its cricket in one of professional sport's saddest human stories. For its part, Somerset and its warm-hearted cricket lovers will never reject him.*

Perish the thought, but David would have been eminently justified in writing those first two sentences about himself. For all their banter and cameraderie, press boxes can be cold, bitchy, back-stabbing places. That's what you get when you deprive a room of fresh oxygen and sensible women. A cricket press box is the most agreeable by a mile: partly because our branch of journalism generally attracts a specific sort of person (patient, contemplative, romantic, irretrievably boyish and often quite potty); partly because, since we spend so many successive hours in cramped conditions away from our nearest and dearest (confirmed bachelors and divorcees are ten a penny), we have no choice but to tolerate each other's idiosyncrasies and peccadilloes. Yet all is not sweetness and light. One former correspondent dangled another out of a Caribbean window by his legs. I can also think of at least two esteemed members of the corps who decline to acknowledge my presence. In the fifteen years I have been frequenting this den of sometime iniquity, however, I have never once heard David referred to with anything other than extreme fondness. He reminds us of the way we would like to be. The way we should be.

By way of expressing his admiration and undying affection, Frank Keating offered an example of his fellow West Countryman's kindness and generosity of spirit. On a regular basis, David, now in his seventieth year himself, hikes over from Westbury-on-Trym near Bristol to the Malvern borders to visit Andy

Wilson, Gloucestershire's much-loved stumper either side of World War II, now seeing out the years alone at his home, *Keeper's Cottage*. David, typically, saw no need to bother me with such apparent trifles.

Keating does. 'Time and again he'll ring me and say, "Are you coming to George's funeral?" (meaning George Lambert) or "Are you coming to Sam's funeral?" (meaning Sam Cook). In a way, by staying in touch with these old players, helping them, paying his respects, he represents all journalists. He's a very special man.'

BASTILLE DAY AT Cheltenham College and the Gloucestershire seamers are guillotining the Sussex top order. Another season of unexpected quality; another summer of eventual discontent. 'I've been told I have a suicide complex,' says David, giggling gingerly. 'Most of my books,' he continues in that soft, genteel, self-deprecating tenor, 'have been about people who have either committed suicide or been on the point of killing themselves, which may suggest a slightly warped personality. I hope not, but ... I'm writing about someone I'm desperately interested in, someone with a complicated life. I'm fairly complicated myself. If there was a war, even though I'm a pacifist, I'd be one of the first to sign on. I wouldn't have the courage to be a conscientious objector.'

Compassionate, I propose, would be a more accurate description of his personality than warped. 'I think that's the nicest compliment anyone can pay me. I'd like to think I am. And that perhaps comes from my background. My parents were simple country people with very strict standards, and I'd like to think those standards have been instilled into me. We might have had the wireless on but nobody ever spoke at our dinner table. I never learned the art of conversation. Which is probably why I write.'

David hails from a long line of Somerset gamekeepers. His grandfather ran twenty miles each night to court his girlfriend, a chambermaid at Sherborne Castle. Both parents were in service at the local manor. After attending the village primary in East Coker he won a scholarship to Yeovil Grammar, cycling there and back but having eyes only for English. Fortunately, his English master had a yen for cricket. He left at sixteen to join the *Western Gazette* as a copy-boy, a period captured graphically and wrily in *Country Reporter*, his acclaimed 'eighty-five per cent autobiographical' novel. Proceeding to the *Bristol Evening World* as a general news reporter in 1955, he switched to a blend of sports reporting and sub-editing in 1958, enabling him to cover Gloucestershire and Somerset home fixtures; forty years on, he is still pounding that same West Country beat. Since 'pounding' is such an inapposite word for a man with so dainty a tread, better make that skipping.

On one indelible occasion he even lived out every sportswriter's secret fantasy/phobia. 'Gloucestershire used to be the big attraction at an annual Bristol six-a-side tournament, all very competitive. They were let down by somebody at the last minute and Tony Brown, the skipper, asked me to make up the numbers. All the team, keeper apart, had to bowl an over – and nothing could be loose. Brown had never seen my bland off-breaks. I panicked, conscious that they would be carted. "When do you want me to bowl?" I asked with quivering voice. "You're not," said Brown. "You'll be the wicketkeeper." I'd never gone behind the stumps in my life – and Mike Procter was one of the bowlers! I stood well back. It went blissfully; nothing got past the bat. And it was a joy to discover that a county fielder's return came straight into the gloves.' More joyous still was his final game for the Bristol Badgers, the homeless club he ran in between assignments. Opening with his son Mark, he put on 'a modest but imperishable stand of 48. Which is probably the only statistic he can remember.'

When the *Bristol Evening World* closed in 1962 – his 'terminal payment' amounted to £280 – he resolved to go freelance, to have a bash on his own, to 'stretch creatively, at least privately'. 'Footie could have gone anywhere in Fleet Street,' recalls Keating, who worked with him on the *Evening World*. 'But even then, that contented rusticity was already there.'

The timing was not opportune. 'We were buying a house and Anne was eight months preggers. I didn't have a single contract or promise of work. But I've always rather liked an element of risk. The artistic elbow-room appealed. I was fed up with being chased by news editors, going on stories I knew were never going to make it. I liked the idea of keeping my own professional diary and going on jobs I had initiated. I liked working from home, in a converted attic, surrounded by 2000 sports books and badly-filed newspaper cuttings. I have loads of self-discipline, and I've always been pushed by the work ethic, emanating from my feudal village days. I'm also very much a loner, though I need friends and journalistic badinage, which I love. I should loathe the relentless and soulless spirit of the modern newspaper office. I've long reached the age when I can stay "stuff it" to that.'

Diversity was another lure. In the mid-Sixties, indeed, he flirted with comedy. Encouraged when a few sketches tickled funny bones on TV, friends suggested he tout himself around. Offering his services to an up-and-coming impersonator named Mike Yarwood, hotfoot from a stint at the Bristol Hippodrome, he was brusquely ignored. Yet when push came to shove, and a not obviously gifted act by the equally unpromising name of Freddie 'Parrot Face' Davies asked him to give up everything to concoct his gags, he got cold feet.

'The *London Evening News* was making a push in Bristol when the *Evening World* shut down, so I covered the courts every day for them, did a bit of ghastly trade journalism and eventually did some part-time subbing and reporting for the

BBC.' There were regular items for *Woman's Hour* and the *Today Programme*; for TWW, its successor HTV and the BBC (for whom daughter Julia, another journo, now works as a senior researcher). He researched and scripted documentaries on anything from gambling to those aforementioned adhesive addicts. Then came a 'horrid' stint of early-morning news bulletins for BBC West and later local radio. 'I'm hopeless with technology. Twice put the station off the air!'

He had already spent a number of years freelancing for *The Guardian*, reviewing first-nights at Bristol's Hippodrome, Theatre Royal and Old Vic, when, in the early Seventies, an opportunity arose to cover county cricket for a national audience, for a paper that would give that elegantly sagacious pen room to flourish (no simple matter when your allotment is 400 words and 23 wickets have tumbled). Fully four decades had passed since David had huddled up next to his father on the bus to Yeovil, willing the rain away en route to watching Somerset take on the might of Lancashire at the local aircraft ground. The most striking and lasting impression had been the sight of Bill Andrews and Arthur Wellard leaving the field at stumps, arms draped matily around each other's shoulders. The press box proved no less refreshing.

'The thing I love is the kinship. I love having a pint with my mates. Out of, say, twenty regular county reporters, I'd consider eighteen to be friends, and share the same feelings. I find most of them, whatever the public's perception, have a great affection for the game. Most of us are, very loosely, frustrated novelists. We all like words, don't we? The first thing my wife will say to me when I get home is: "Was it a good box today?" Apart from the advent of the laptop it hasn't changed much down the years. We're bloody privileged to be covering county cricket because it's an anachronism. And I don't think it'll be around for much longer. It's been by far the most pleasurable part of my career.

'The one pity is that the players now are terribly defensive. There isn't an affinity at all, I don't think. I suppose the tabloids have something to answer for. It isn't all their fault. I've worked for them and I'm not against sensationalism in all cases – like reporting an outbreak of VD during the war – but the tabloids are reprehensible sometimes. Though no more so than some famous sportsmen I could mention. I can think of many who have been shielded by journalists.'

It took a while for him to shed that innate reticence. 'It wasn't until late in life that I discovered that I could be slightly interpretative. Until then my life as a journalist had been utterly objective. I went to a police court or a coroner's court or a council meeting, where you listen to the words of someone else. I was dissuaded from expressing an opinion, which fits nicely with my personality because I haven't got a great point of view. I'm rather proud of this. I don't say it boastfully, but … you can opt out of life so easily if you haven't got a very strong point of view. Then I discovered I could be more expansive a) with theatre, and b), with cricket and sport. In an odd way, sport allows opinion, and I know what I approve of and what I disapprove of, but I wouldn't want to write about it *ad infinitum*. I'm also desperately uninterested in the politics of cricket. Lord MacLaurin means nothing to me. Two divisions means nothing to me. Perhaps it's my age. Perhaps that's why I'd never have made a cricket correspondent even if I had started earlier. Maybe I'm too bland. My wife's a magistrate – maybe this is why I could never be one. I can be so easily seduced by opposing points of view and I end up not knowing which way to go and I allow my emotions to guide me. But I'm a fairly contemplative person, not a white-hot person, which is why being a correspondent wouldn't have been right for me. In cricket, if you like, I take the coward's way out.' Nelson Mandela should have such a yellow streak.

HAD HE NEVER written a single book, David would still have performed a service of inestimable value to the discerning cricket aficionado. Cobbled together from scrawled notes in the margins of that day's *Guardian* or *Times*, roughed out on a pad of A4 and largely ad-libbed to the copytaker, there is about his reporting an unerring sense of timelessness, understated at their romantic core yet wholly seductive. Unlike some writers not too far from this keyboard, he has no affinity for 'polishing'. And even less for hi-tech. 'It's probably my age,' he admits needlessly (and not for the first time), 'but I am very wary and cynical about progress.'

On the day Brian Lara scored his record-shattering 501 David reckons he was the only reporter at Edgbaston not to have his knickers twisted when the computer systems went down: he had filed two 900-word pieces before many of the others had transmitted a word. Which gave him an appreciable kick. 'It's the irony,' he chuckles gently, 'the irony of progress.' Articles, essays and books are composed on a battered typewriter in his converted attic back in Westbury-on-Trym, complete with faint h's and dodgy t's. The sole concession to modernity is a mobile phone. Perhaps he is convinced that nothing significant ever changes? It would certainly account for that timeless aura.

Maybe the proximity of the cathedral affected Surrey. They put Gloucestershire in, when play eventually started after lunch on the second day, and punctuated the afternoon with mighty and melodious appeals fit to clinch any chorister's audition. As a team at the top they are understandably jaunty and hungry. The ground looked a treat, pleasing for the King's School headmaster Peter Lacey – who now waits to discover how longstanding this county venue will be – and the pupils who came to watch in mid-afternoon. But the wicket was never too easy. Some of the early batsmen were left peering at the strip as if, unreasonably, it held subterranean horrors in keeping with the city's current tales of the macabre.

I defy you to place that report in time (the place was Gloucester, though it could just as easily have been any one of a myriad of county outgrounds). Only David could make 1994 sound like 1954. Or vice versa. Reared though he was on the deeds of Hutton and Hammond, and unlike so many of his generation, he rejoices in the present. 'I don't think I'm blasé. I'm a great enthusiast, and I've retained that enthusiasm for the game. Mind you, the generation gap is a disadvantage. I got on so well with the Somerset players when I started reporting but I find it more difficult now. And it's probably because they look at me and think, "That old man reminds me of my grandfather". Which is valid, absolutely valid.'

True, he was fortunate that, between them, Somerset and Gloucestershire, for all their interminable struggles – neither has won an official championship title – have boasted several of the most singular talents to grace the modern game. It is more than mere coincidence, however, that despite the fact that he was twice their age, he won the trust of three dazzling stars from wildly contrasting constellations: Cheshire's Ian Botham, Antigua's Viv Richards and Karachi's Zaheer Abbas. Serving as a ghost for the last two was his entrée to more personal projects, as well as the source of many an indelible image and insight.

Here is Zaheer in Lahore, early 1983, shortly after that graceful, voracious Pakistani had notched twin centuries in a match for the eighth time, outstripping Fry, Bradman and Hammond:

When he joined Gloucestershire in 1972 he spoke few English words. He is now efficiently bi-lingual. 'You know how important that innings was to me. Whenever I am scoring runs I am happy. I crack one record and am already looking for the next.' There is no swagger in the way he says it. We chatted and then he snoozed in the treatment room – in a pattern which I found endearing. He isn't physically strong and has had problems with his health over the past year or so. You wouldn't think so as he rises on his toes to produce the best square-cut in current cricket. 'See you back in England,' he waves. I edge uneasily past the armed police – one of whom stops me from taking some innocuous holiday cine film as if I were a fugitive from a le Carré novel – and I know indisputedly in my heart that the bat is mightier than the gun.

And here is Botham, Taunton '85, at the start of his last bodacious summer:

His teammates, who like all county cricketers can be sparing in their praise, say their captain has never played better; he's back to the form of the richest years in that cussed and contradictory career of his. He's nimbler than he has been for a long time, belying the rural sturdiness of the waist. He has more zest too, and his England place is what he, as a racing man, might call a cast-iron cert. The blond hair tops a face of buoyant challenge.

'I'm not sure whether Both and Viv were good for each other,' muses David hesitantly, anxious not to cause offence. 'I had a particularly good relationship with Viv, possibly as close as anyone on the circuit, largely because, when he was at Taunton in his early days, I was working for the BBC and doing all his early broadcasts back to the Caribbean. That gave us a strong bond. The arrogance, as some see it, is partly a cover. He's got fierce racial pride but he always used to wish he was more articulate. He probably is, now, but at the time I think he was aware that he wasn't in the same league, in that respect, as many of the other players. I also think he was envious of Botham's bravado. There was an inter-rivalry; they played off each other. Viv tried to match Both, which was never really on because they were so disparate as people. I'm getting away from the cricket again, aren't I?

'I'm not just interested in the drama of runs and wickets. I've always been aware that one of the disciplines of journalism is to disguise emotion but I'm much more interested, and get privately excited, if I hear a bat going through a dressing-room window, or I see two players having a row, or I see one in turmoil because he's had five ducks in a row. Or I see one in tears, as I do occasionally, because he's not getting a new contract. Or when one has his fifteen minutes of glory. That thrills me. You know he's not going to get a new contract but he has this wonderful game, or takes this wonderful catch that lights up the whole afternoon. That still thrills me.'

NO ONE, THOUGH, has thrilled him more than Gimblett. 'He was my hero. He was everything I'd like to have been. He was the romantic batsman who'd hit sixes in the first over. His bat was always smiling. He was the smiling cricketer. Then I began to discover the paradoxes, and I realised he didn't smile much at all. That's what fascinated me. I fell in love, fell out of love, then, at the end, fell back in love again. The book wrote itself.'

Did Gimblett see cricket as a means of disguise, of avoiding his true self? 'Maybe, but then Harold claimed to despise the game. He told me so often he hated it. He hated playing for England. He prayed they'd never select him again – he only won three caps, y'know. There was the psychosomatic business of the carbuncle on his neck the last time he was picked. It was almost as if he imagined it. He said he didn't want to be a cricketer, but in retrospect we know that's a lie, because he was so richly gifted.

'There was a tremendous misery and mental instability in the family. His father had a mental problem; his son was a quite agonised young man. It was a long line of unhappiness. There were the complexes about money, about status: Harold went to a minor public school. It was the sheer riddle of the man that fascinated me.

Above: Cap town... Ali Bacher sweeps Fred Titmus during the third Test at The Oval, 1965; Colin Cowdrey and Jim Parks wish they had time to admire
(*Hulton Getty*)

Right: The persuader (1)... Ali reasons with riot police during the last 'rebel' tour of South Africa, 1990 (*Simon Bruty/ Allsport*)

The persuader (2)... Ali with Sir Gary Sobers on a visit to Soweto, June 1991 (*Shaun Botterill/ Allsport*)

On the brink... Ali, now managing director of the United Cricket Board of South Africa, addresses the 1991 ICC meeting at Lord's that approved his country's restoration to the fold (*Shaun Botterill/Allsport*)

Fresh fields...Ali with India's Mohammad Azharuddin after South Africa had won their first one-day international, New Delhi, November 1991 (*Shaun Botterill/Allsport*)

Dove affair... Ali (far right) enthuses as Azharuddin releases the perennial peace symbols before the start of South Africa's first post-apartheid Test, Durban 1992 (*Patrick Eagar*)

'I got to know him particularly well during a Benson and Hedges game for which he was adjudicating the Gold Award. I'd taken a dislike to him during his days as coach and groundsman at Millfield, when a colleague wrote something critical of his pitch and he came to the press box and rather pompously said he didn't like it. But that day I found him walking outside the ground, not really adjudicating at all. He didn't have the courage to make a decision. We had a long chat about that and our friendship seemed to develop from that point. Then he asked me to help him with the book he was writing. Then he lost interest; then he killed himself. Then a relative of his rang and said, "I think you should know – he left you some tapes". I've still got them, and I treasure them. A lot of people say they'd love them and I say, "You'll never get 'em".'

If Gimblett's story wrote itself, the similarly poignant saga of Walter Reginald Hammond, one of the most brilliant cricketers of his or any other generation, was assembled, shaped and planed over half a lifetime. 'I never met him. Only saw him bat twice or three times at most, but he was someone I'd wanted to write about for forty years. Normally I write very quickly – three or four months for a book usually – but that one, the research, the stored-away memories, took forty years from the moment I was first told of his illness, in confidence. I kept it to myself. I knew the source was absolutely impeccable; and I got it confirmed from three other sources. But that was just the starting point. The fact that Wally had a "social disease" means nothing to me. There are a million things worse than catching a dose.'

Hammond had other substantial disadvantages. Frowned upon as a professional, he was obliged to turn amateur in order to captain his country. Then there were those murmurings about 'gypsy blood'. Worse, so far as he was concerned, his peak – 1928 to 1938 – coincided with that of one Donald George Bradman: keen as the rivalry was, more pleasing as the Englishman's strokes were, Hammond knew he could never outstrip the Australian phenomenon. His only consolation was to rob him of the highest individual score in Tests; even then, a Yorkshireman filched his thunder. The sense of failure was acute. It may explain the helpless philandering.

David's principal contention, based on medical advice, is that Hammond may well have suffered mercury poisoning while undergoing treatment for his affliction, which would explain the mood swings and paranoias that perplexed so many. 'I was very fearful of the reaction because I didn't like Wally at all while I was writing it, though by the end I liked him very much indeed. It sounds patronising but I felt desperately sorry for him. The loneliness at the end, the unfulfilled man. Living in South Africa, virtually penniless, forgotten, he believed, by the establishment here, never given the knighthood others had been given. Now I'm very against knighthoods but he had a case.

'It's not a salacious book at all. I've only had two complaints. One was a letter, I suspect from an academic, writing about an extract that appeared in *Wisden Cricket Monthly*. A very unpleasant man, talking about my integrity. It was a very unfair letter. How dare I write about Wally Hammond when I didn't know him! Very very pompous. And there was someone in Bristol, who used to be on the Gloucestershire committee. "I've just read your book," he said to me. "Oh – what do you think of it?" I replied. "I hated it," he said. But I had 250 complimentary letters, the most I've ever had. I've kept most of them. A lot said it was a compassionate book, that it was written with affection.'

WHEN THE WORDS aren't flowing up in that chock-a-block den in Westbury-on-Trym, David reaches for a cricket ball: 'I use it like a set of worry-beads'. Alternatively, he'll turn to his 'therapies'. He may wander into his vegetable garden, hand-weeding the turnips or thinning the beets. Or sit down at his rickety upright piano, a gift from his parents when he was six. A self-confessed 'frustrated jazz pianist', he is adamant he hasn't improved technically since his first lesson ('I have all the shoulder motions of the definitive jazz pianist and absolutely none of the skills'). Not that that prevents him from tinkling *Sunrise Sunset* and adding a touch of syncopation. Or experimenting with Gershwin, a fellow dab hand at rhapsodies in blue. Far from the maddening crowd.

'Village life is so important to me. I love the pace. I love the fact that people say "good morning". I love the gardens. I went back to East Coker last weekend. For so many of the villagers there the garden was their only creative outlet. My father was so pedantic about his straight lines of onions and carrots. A creative exercise for non-artistic people. I found that joyful.' Here, quite evidently, and in vast dissimilarity to his subjects, is a chap at peace: with himself, with his muse, with his world.

The next project is another delve into the psyches of his idols, from pugilist Jack 'Kid' Berg and rugger bugger Carwyn James to that fountain of cricketing pith and wisdom, Raymond Charles ('RC') Robertson-Glasgow, of Charterhouse, Oxford University, Somerset and *The Observer*. Along with a rather better-known Raymond (Chandler of that ilk), 'Crusoe' – who as *Wisden* so delicately phrased it, 'died suddenly' – was David's literary role model. 'I met him once, at the press box at Taunton. Again, suicide. Manic depressive.' Cue guilty smirk. 'Drawn to the subject yet again.' Like Freud to a bed-wetter.

'I'd put Crusoe ahead of Cardus. Cardus was a wonderful writer but his allusions were far too obscure for me. And, I suspect, slightly phoney at times. You've got to be envious of someone who can write so well but Crusoe was my man. Humanity. Unpretentious.' The baton could not be in safer hands.

Chapter 7: The Administrator's Tale

'Grace, who is a very good asker of questions, asked Ali what his motivation was. And he said, "I think because I'm a Jew". My respect for him grew because I felt that was a genuine answer. There was that conviction.'

David Sheppard on Ali Bacher

BREAKFAST-TIME at The Waldorf Hotel, second morning of the Lord's Test, 1998. Dr Ali Bacher pops a couple of mysterious-looking pills and bolts back some orange juice. 'Morning, Brian,' he chirps, spotting Brian McMillan's villainous jaw hovering over the never-ending buffet. South Africa's once-indomitable all-rounder is now an idle, frustrated reserve; Ali is eager to keep peckers up. 'Keep on going, all right?'

Shortly afterwards, while Ali is asserting that the International Cricket Council's movers and shakers are a distinct improvement on their predecessors ('qualified people are coming through'), Hansie Cronje, McMillan's captain, moseys towards the bacon with purposeful tread.

'Captain,' exclaims Ali, 'how are you?' Cronje interrupts his quest and repairs to our table. 'Well batted yesterday,' enthuses Ali. 'It's going to be a good day, captain. Just control your number six, will you?' Cue hearty cackle. Cronje smirks bashfully. 'Tell him it's not a thirty-over game,' quips Ali, grinning the soft, indulgent grin of the understanding parent. Of cricket's very own Godfather.

RUMINATING ON ALI'S high-flying, turbulence-packed reign as captain of South Africa, Mike Procter, arguably the brightest cricketing star to be dimmed by apartheid, praised him as 'a shrewd puller of strings'. Seldom, though, has even this accomplished puppeteer had to pull quite so many quite so shrewdly.

It would not be stretching things overmuch to suggest that, as managing director of the United Cricket Board of South Africa and chairman of the ICC Development Committee, Ali, now a vigorous fifty-six, holds the future of the game in his hands. The brief, as he sees it, is to reinvent it in South Africa as 'the People's Game' and ensure its wider future via that buzziest of contemporary cricketing buzzwords, 'globalisation'. Procter wasn't exaggerating all that much when he described him as the bravest man in the Republic.

'Dr Bacher,' pronounced that most courageous of his countrymen, Nelson Mandela, '*is* South Africa.' There was a time, of course, when such testimony would have been entirely derogatory. While the foremost symbol of the anti-apartheid movement was languishing on Robben Island, lest we forget, Ali, at the behest of those profoundly unenlightened despots in the National Government, was offering the world's finest cricketers substantial sums to contravene the United Nations-sanctioned sports boycott, a political tool whose importance in the destruction of apartheid should never be underestimated. Things change. And how.

In twinning Ali and South Africa, Mandela was presumably referring to the mutual contradictions as well as the mutual ambitions. Yet for all one's reservations about those sanctions-busting 'rebel' tours Ali orchestrated during the Eighties (he claims he underwent 'a Damascan conversion' during the last such venture in 1989), the sheer zeal and dedication with which he tackles the game's most pressing and problematic issues are nothing if not persuasive.

His priority, not unnaturally, lies squarely with his homeland. Without him, the game in the Rainbow Nation would still be strictly monochrome, still riven by the siege mentality and branded prejudices that have left those Afrikaaner rugger-buggers in such a pitiful state. He acknowledges that inconsistencies remain, that work aplenty is required before South Africa can field a representative XI with any pretence of proportional representation, let alone verisimilitude. Ahead lay calls from the ANC for at least one black player to be included in every national XI, a short-sighted if understandable response to a fiendishly awkward situation. Ahead, too, lay the brinkmanship that would rescue the inaugural tour of the Republic by an official West Indies party. Delayed by squabbles over money in the Caribbean, the most significant sporting visitation in South African history – potentially – owed its eventual existence to Ali the Diplomat at his most disarmingly persuasive. The point is, he has shown what is possible, that meaningful progress can be made. For that alone he deserves gratitude. Not to say forgiveness.

MAKHAYA NTINI, THE young black fast bowler whose action is the very spit of Malcolm Marshall, whose selection for the tour is seen by many as having had as much to do with politics as ability, comes over to pay his respects. Ali shakes his hand warmly, turns to a colleague, yet continues to hang on to those long, branch-like fingers. Hanging on to the future.

Now and again during our conversation, Ali the Family Man pops up. At Lord's the previous afternoon, he readily confesses, he had been 'a bag of nerves' while Dominic Cork was administering a thorough going-over to nephew Adam (whom I shamefully cite as his son; a common boob, he assures me). 'He's my son when he's doing well,' chuckles Uncle Ali. 'Clyde Walcott feels he plays too much on the front foot.' Concern is writ large.

Quietly-spoken, as if conscious that that clipped Jo'burg twang might alienate sensitive English ears, to spend any decent length of time with the world's best-known gynaecologist is to be convinced that he *cares* about cricket. Passionately. Even forty-five minutes will do. Consummate politician he may be, supreme opportunist he may be, but at least he has a worthy cause. And tenacity to match.

When I note that the structure of the limited-overs game could learn much from baseball – especially the frequent rotation of innings – the riposte would have done Lord Snooty proud: 'To sell the game to the Americans we'll probably have to come up with a game that lasts three to three and a half hours [the length of a longish baseball game], which is why we've just merged Australia's Super Eights and New Zealand's Cricket Max. And we're [the UCB] introducing split innings in our domestic one-day tournament next year. But cricket's a better game, a much better game than baseball.'

BETWEEN DIVERSIONS WE conduct a whistle-stop tour of the full life and seldom tribulation-free times of Dr Aron Bacher, the first doctor to captain a Test side since good ol' WG and arguably the most important sportsman ever to spring from Jewish loins.

Helpfully, his parents fled Lithuania a couple of years before the Holocaust, enabling him to grow up in an environment rather more conducive to athletic pursuits. Dubbed 'Ali' by a pal when he was nine (after the well-known thief), he spent most of his formative years on a farm outside Johannesburg. The Bachers were a sporty lot. Uncle Aaron bowled inswingers for Transvaal; Ali's brothers played squash and hockey at a high level. Tennis was his first love until he was fourteen, whereupon lack of headway prompted a switch to cricket. 'I bowled leg-breaks but they were pretty ordinary. I didn't drop the bowling; it dropped me.'

Within a year he was turning out for the first XI of a prominent Jo'burg club, Balfour Park. He could scarcely have wished for a more searching initiation. Among his adversaries were bowlers of such fearsome repute as Neil Adcock, still regarded by many as South Africa's finest fast bowler, and Hugh Tayfield, the only truly great spinner ever to sport a Springbok on his chest. The experience did not go unappreciated.

Entering medical school at eighteen, he juggled with rare assurance. Selected to play for Transvaal against M.J.K. Smith's English tourists in the southern hemisphere summer of 1964–65, he contrived to have his exams brought forward. In another respect the blinkers were tugged tight. In his teens he had played in a game amid the spartan confines of the Natalspuit Indian sports ground, between a team led by ex-Springbok skipper John Waite and a combined black Transvaal XI – and finished on the losing side. There were, needless to add, no toasts of mutual admiration in the bar.

'The following day nobody wondered why we didn't do this all the time,' Ali would reflect. 'We didn't ask, do they have any facilities, do they have any money or sponsorship? If I regret one attitude of my life in the Sixties it is this. I used to vote for the Progressive [anti-apartheid] party but I still played in front of segregated crowds in Newlands and Wanderers [a bastion of privilege much like Lord's, only more so] with the blacks sitting in cages in the hottest part of the ground. I just didn't think about it. That was the terrible thing.'

Dark and tousled of hair, slight of frame and often mistaken for the retiring sort, Ali belonged to the most illustrious generation of cricketers his nation had ever possessed. Correct, purposeful and aware of his limitations, Ali the batsman was considered one of the lesser mortals, even though his 235 for Transvaal against the Australians in 1966 set a new mark for the highest score made against a touring team on South African soil. Hewn from much the same rock was John Traicos, the erudite, pencil-thin, Egyptian-born off-spinner who would still be Zimbabwe's leading bowler deep into his forties. Rabble-rousing Eddie Barlow and cool Trevor Goddard were the older hands, gifted all-rounders both yet positively humdrum by comparison with Procter, the only jack-of-all-tradesman worthy of mention in the same breath as Sobers.

There were the Pollock brothers: Peter, purveyor of bouncers and yorkers for the cognescenti, and Graeme, willow wielder to the Gods, rated by no less a sage than Bradman as the most resplendent left-handed batsman of them all. Given the opportunity – he played in but twenty-three Tests – does Ali think the younger Pollock had it in him to go the extra yard and average 70, say? 'Yes. He was a genius. He was born like that. He hit on the up, scored quickly. Only one of his ilk comes along every hundred years.' And then there was Barry Richards, whose four Test caps constituted scandalous reward for an opener of such heavenly magnitude.

'My claim to fame,' asserts Ali, grinning slyly, 'is that I kept Barry out of the series against Australia in 1966–67. I batted at number three and he couldn't get in. The selectors wanted continuity after beating England in 1965. I kept chipping away so they didn't drop me. We didn't know how good he [Richards] was going to be. I asked Bradman how good he was and he said he was as good as Hutton and Hobbs.' Sport's loss may ultimately have been humanity's gain, but the sense of deprivation was still acute.

For a while, all went swimmingly for Ali; South Africa, too (the non-coloured sections, that is). The Republic had been expelled from the Olympic movement as well as the (then) Imperial Cricket Conference, but the remaining white constituents of the Test fraternity – England, Australia and New Zealand – were still eminently willing to play ball. Given that it was ever thus, apartheid, to all intents and purposes, had actually had no impact on cricket in the Republic whatsoever.

In one respect, Ali was unfortunate to tour England in the summer of 1965. Blue skies were thinner on the ground than black smiles in Rhodesia, where the National Front party, arch-proponents of white rule, had just made sweeping gains in the elections. The new boy coped admirably, finishing second in the overall averages to Pollock Minor with 1008 runs at 40.32, including 67 in the second Test and 70 in the third. His most celebrated moment came at Leicester, where he and off-spinner Jackie Botten added 181 in 137 minutes, then a ninth-wicket record for any South African collective outside terra familiar. Unperturbed by what few demonstrations there were, Peter van de Merwe's side took the series one–nil, thanks almost exclusively to Pollock Minor's exceptional 125 on a decidedly seamer-friendly pitch at Trent Bridge. In the seventy minutes after lunch on the first day, having entered at 16 for two and subsequently seen the total wither to 80 for five, the young colossus scored 91 out of 102, defying reporters of all ages to summon suitable superlatives.

Australia, visitors to the Cape in 1966–67, supplied the next array of necks for the chopping-block. Beaten three–one in the Tests – it would have been four–one had the elements desisted for another half-an-hour at The Wanderers. It was the first time an Australian party had ever been beaten in an overseas series outside the Motherland. The Springbok was the cock of the walk. For the first time, the world's best white cricket team was devoid of Pom and Cobber.

The cancellation of the 1968–69 MCC tour was a bitter blow, yet the Australian selectors remained untroubled by decisions of a racial nature and their nominees returned at the end of 1969, to be thrashed four–nil in one of the most one-sided encounters the game has ever served up. Richards, in what would prove to be his only Test series, was simply majestic; Pollock Minor's 274 in Durban established a new benchmark – the highest score for South Africa, surviving for almost three decades until Daryll Cullinan swiped it; Procter, still feeling his way with the bat, opted to destroy with the ball, taking 26 wickets at 13.57. Behind them stood Ali the conductor, keeping the virtuosos in tune. 'I like to deal with people,' he told Henry Blofeld. 'I like to know and try to understand their problems and try to help them. I'm a great believer in team spirit.'

And it showed. As a captain, Procter puts him in the same ballpark as Mike Brearley. 'He was a marvellous motivator who had total respect. He was also lucky. Almost every hunch seemed to come off, especially when he brought on that great partnership-breaker, Eddie Barlow. Eddie always thought he should be bowling – he never was one for self-doubt – and the trick was knowing when to let loose all that aggression. Time and again, he would be brought on and do the necessary. Barlow would get the credit, but Ali was the shrewd puller of strings … the ideal captain of an excellent, strong-willed side. Intelligent enough to encourage lively discussions in the dressing-room, he had the knack of understanding each player's own character. Ali was the nearest to Brearley in that respect.'

Cue reality. The Blofeld interview ran in the June 1970 edition of *The Cricketer*. Publication had been timed to coincide with the arrival of the South African tourists at Heathrow. They never got there, of course. E.W. Swanton's

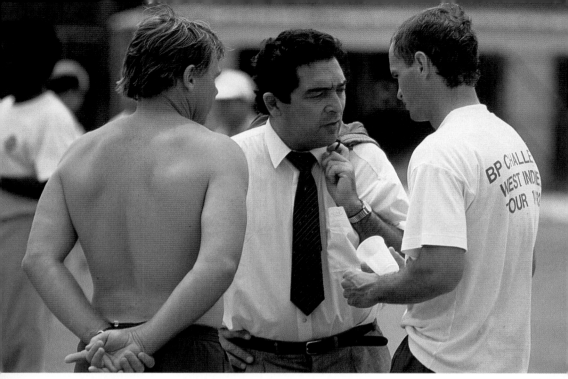

Previous page: Never a lull moment… Ali at London's Waldorf Hotel e*n route* to Lord's for the England–South Africa Test, June 1998. Calls for a fully representative South African team were growing (*Graham Goldwater*)
Above: Bridgetown over troubled water… Ali with Mike Procter (*left*) and Kepler Wessels at the Kensington Oval before South Africa's inaugural Test against the West Indies, Barbados 1992 (*Patrick Eagar*)
Below: Major occasion… John Major concentrates on the action as Ali (*front, second from right*) talks to Mark Baldwin of the Press Association during South Africa's first Test against England for 28 years, Lord's 1994 (*Patrick Eagar*)

No looking back... John Harris, powder-blue umpire's jacket swapped for official ECB employee's blazer, after a Sunday League match at Taunton, September 1998 (*Graham Goldwater*)

Tilling the soil... Bryan Valentine (*left*) and Percy Chapman (*centre*) of Kent and England with John's grandfather, Harry 'Fernie' Ferdinando, Somerset's groundsman for a quarter of a century, at Taunton, *c.*1930 (*John Harris Collection*)

The things we do for love... John, a firm lover of whites, walks out to the middle at Taunton with John Holder (*left*), powder-blue jackets to the fore, September 1998 (*Graham Goldwater*)

Us and them… the two Johns consult after the fall of a wicket, Taunton 1998 (*Graham Goldwater*)

editorial in the same issue makes instructive reading. 'Unless the South African tour has been cancelled between writing and publication, English cricket faces an ordeal the likely character of which must fill all who love the game with the deepest melancholy.' His distress, it should be pointed out, lay with the threats against the tourists issued by the 'Stop the Tour' militants.

The Newlands Walk-Off, as it was termed, provided the first indication that the players were prepared to take a stand in favour of multi-racialism. 'It was frustration with the government,' recalled Procter. 'By April [1971] we were still clinging to the fond hope that we might still be able to tour Australia later that year.' The government's refusal to countenance the South African Cricket Association's proposal that two non-white players be selected was the last straw. 'We decided to walk off [the field] at a certain stage, hand a statement to the press, then go back. Both sets of players agreed and after I had bowled one ball at Barry Richards, we all trooped off.' The statement ran as follows: 'We cricketers feel that the time has come for an expression of our views. We fully support the South African Cricket Association's application to include non-whites on the tour to Australia if good enough, and furthermore, subscribe to merit being the only criterion on the cricket field.' Ali felt it did more harm than good. 'I couldn't go to Newlands but I knew all about it. It was a good gesture but it brought out the anger of the government. At that time, on that type of issue, it couldn't countenance views that conflicted with their ideology.'

Ali, for his part, had rather bigger fish to fry. While working in a multi-racial hospital in Johannesburg – 'at a time,' notes Procter, 'when that wasn't the fashionable thing to do' – he swept up the ladder, becoming South African cricket's leading administrator and reformer. Others, such as Peter Hain, main orchestrator of the 1970 'Stop the Tour' campaign, were sceptical. The pair met at Hain's Putney home during the Seventies, shortly after Hain had suggested to Donald Woods, the journalist, that the only way of ending the boycott was to advise dear old Mr Vorster to amend the Group Areas Act and the Reservation Separate Amenities Act. 'In short,' surmised Woods, 'Vorster would have to take through Parliament a bill which exempted sports from all the apartheid legislation.' To Hain, as Mihir Bose delicately put it in *Sporting Colours – Sport and Politics in South Africa*, Ali was 'acting as some sort of emissary of the white South African cricket body'.

'English-speaking South Africans I've always been suspicious of – even though I was one myself,' admitted Hain many years later. 'Bacher was much more aggressive [than Danie Craven, the Holy Roman Emperor of South African rugby, who had also visited Hain to plead his sport's case]. Basically, he said, "Look, you know, we are doing what we can. You are asking for the impossible." I was not very impressed with Ali, then, and the feeling increased during the rebel tours. In the end, I grant you, he saw the light sooner than anybody else.'

According to Procter, he began this process by dragging his fellow administrators 'towards a closer understanding of non-white frustrations at the lack of facilities and hope. He was brave enough to hand out home truths to the government at a time when it was fashionable to keep your head down.' For all that it was largely cosmetic until the end of apartheid, the township programme stood tallest among the reformer's schemes. By 1986, a State of Emergency had been declared. Where most whites feared reprisals, Ali proclaimed his intention to use cricket as a force to heal, taking it into the most hazardous areas, deploying it to break down barriers. More than 1000 children turned up in Soweto when he went on radio to invite them for a weekend's cricket in a local park. Procter, like many of those not in the know, was in awe.

'Ali admits he was scared when he arrived. He knew there was no trust in the white man in those sprawling ghettos; he was aware that he might be sacrificed. But [he] had a better chance of a rewarding dialogue. He had worked in a hospital in Soweto and his reputation as a fair man wasn't confined to white people in prosperous suburbs. He talked to the black leaders, aware that the order to slit his throat might not be too far away. He talked to black teachers, trying to convince them that a properly organised cricket programme could make their jobs easier and give their pupils some hope. Ali talked and talked, something that comes naturally to him. Some of those township areas were as dangerous and lawless as Beirut. It was no sensible place for a smooth-talking Jewish idealist who had captained white South Africa at cricket.'

In essence, the township programme achieved its aims, taking the game to where it had always been seen as a white man's plaything. Cadbury's financed twenty-one black schools in Transvaal so they could afford to play against their white counterparts (travel and kit included); South African Cricket Union (SACU) officials opened new grounds in Johannesburg, Pretoria, Bloemfontein, Kimberley and East London. The outside world, however, was more concerned with the treatment meted out in Cape Town to Colin Croft, one of the meatier Caribbean catches lured by the bait of the blood-drenched krugerrand.

On a train journey from Newlands to the city centre during the 1984 'rebel' tour, the rangy fast bowler mistakenly sat down in a whites-only carriage and was summarily ejected. When Alvin Kallicharran, his fellow Guyanan, was refused service in a Johannesburg burger bar while playing for Transvaal, he shrugged his shoulders; Croft was less compliant. 'Croft tested the system on purpose,' claimed Peter Cooke, the South African record producer whose persuasive tongue helped Ali convince the seemingly unattainable likes of Geoff Boycott and Graham Gooch to risk bans by joining the first band of mercenaries in 1982. 'He [Ali] was a highly intelligent man and things were being exposed, the window dressing was going, the shop was starting to crumble.'

How optimistic was Ali that attitudes would soften? 'In the late Sixties, fairly, but by the late Seventies the writing was on the wall. Doug Insole [former Essex captain-turned-TCCB bigwig and roving ambassador-cum-schmoozer] would always encourage us. "Don't worry," he'd say. "Keep on going." Although we never actually attended, we always came to London for the annual ICC meeting. Insole told me that England and Australia really wanted to play us but they daren't.'

Did he feel as if he were banging his head against a wall of Berlinesque pro-portions? 'No, I never felt that way. You can't. You love the game. So you play it or administer it to the best of your ability. Life goes on. Cricket was unfairly targeted – but I can't say unfairly because it was right. We *had* to get the poli-tics right. We didn't deserve to play.'

AMID ALL THESE recollections, fond and otherwise, came a rather startling confession. About how, on his Test debut at Lord's in 1965, his approach had verged on the frivolous. 'Almost went first ball. Went just over middle stump. The occasion got the better of me ... I was very nervous but I went to the oppo-site extreme. I talked myself into looking at it another way. When I went out there I was almost flippant.'

To envisage the game's most accomplished wheeler-dealer behaving with anything remotely resembling rashness demands a leap of the imagination even the creators of Superman might have baulked at. That said, Ali is the first to admit it was not his last error of judgment. Impetuosity, kindled by that unquenchable fire, has not always been his friend. And he certainly recognises the folly of those 'rebel' tours. 'Bacher has two qualities rare amongst his white South African contemporaries,' warranted Mihir Bose. 'He is ready to own up to responsibility for past actions and he is a great learner.'

So why piss everyone off in the first place? 'We wanted to regenerate the game in South Africa,' replies Ali, trying hard to disguise the fact that he has just been asked this very question for the umpteenth-and-first time. 'Some form of international competition, if not Tests, to motivate the players and draw crowds. Bringing over the West Indians, Sri Lankans and English did have the desired effect over a period of time but, in retrospect, it was wrong. We never realised the extent of the anger of the black people.

'We were living in a cocoon. The blacks couldn't demonstrate. When they were allowed to do so, on Mike Gatting's tour in 1989, only then did we realise the depth of anger. I was in a terrible situation. It was a very unhappy time, very unhappy. The demonstrators made their feelings quite clear. To me, to everyone. You had to get permission to demonstrate, to march, from a magistrate. But at Kimberley the magistrate turned the application down. So I pushed him and pushed him to let it go on. I facilitated the march! Crazy.

'We realised we couldn't go on after two or three matches. Gatting and his men were due to go down to Cape Town. We were lucky nobody had been killed yet. So we called a board meeting and that was it. There were seven guidelines regarding cancellation and I went beyond them. I also cancelled the second tour [scheduled for the following year]. I just knew that was the last time we'd have a rebel tour. I conceded that right away.' Does he regard the sports boycott as a positive strategy? 'Definitely. A very clever strategy. It preyed on the South African love of sport.'

David Sheppard shelved his scepticism during that whistlestop tour of the townships. 'The Gatting tour was just over when I visited and I regretted they went. But meeting Ali changed my mind about him. I felt he wasn't just acting in the interests of the South African Cricket Union. He was very, very committed. In Tembisa our hosts insisted that we must come to a reception and tea, before we could go and watch the cricket. A woman greeted us. She likened The Wanderers ground in Johannesburg – where the most promising boys were taken for further coaching – to heaven, and Ali to the Messiah. Clearly she saw cricket as the way for a black boy to get out of the townships – but Ali Bacher as the Messiah! He got a bit embarrassed by that.'

AND SO TO the present. If the garden is not quite rosy, it has certainly had a mighty good weeding. Apartheid is history, Mandela is president, South Africa are back in the fold, Ntini has become the first black African to represent the Republic on a cricket field, and Ali is still tugging those strings. Nobody could have done more to help sport find normality in an ocean of abnormality. The pace of progress has been astonishing, yet chinks, understandably, remain.

Does Ali also concede – as he was reported to have done at the press conference following the ICC's 1998 Lord's conflab – that critical errors were made in the constitution of the UCB, which these days purports to represent cricket in the Republic and yet whose executive board, at the time of writing, numbered but one black representative? 'The papers didn't record that properly. Things *aren't* perfect. The imbalance *is* too great. One of the flaws in the constitution was only having one black African on the board. We need more at the highest level. And now we're going to have three. But I don't think that was an error. We just need to be more proactive, to go in a different direction.'

From that same press conference came a curious statement that encapsulated South Africa's dilemma. Domestic leagues, Ali averred, 'should' have more non-white teams, 'but not must'. Standards must not, cannot, be compromised. But surely the ends – the 'People's Game' he so craves – will justify the means?

'It's a fine balancing act, a very fine balancing act. We *mustn't* compromise standards. But if I was a selector I'd pick a young bloke over an old one. I'd also want to give the black guy a chance. They need more opportunities. Paul Adams [the bullish young coloured spinner] has been bowling unbelievably well. He can do a lot of good. Ntini too. They're the future.'

SO WHAT OF the game at large as it approaches the millennium? Idealism and realism, as ever, are on collision course. 'It's too narrowly confined. Big numbers play, particularly on the Indian sub-continent, but when you talk about high profile – government support, media support, sponsor support ...' Words momentarily fail him. 'Holland have been playing for a hundred years but they only have 5000 cricketers. Ireland have 9000. In many of these countries the expatriates play, not the indigenous peoples. *That's* the challenge. The USA, China.'

Does he really consider it feasible to sell the nuances of Test cricket to those unconnected to the umbilical cord of Commonwealth and Empire? 'No. You'd be crazy to try and take Test cricket to the USA. You can't really sell it. But you can have different products for different markets. In April last year we met with senior people from Atlanta. We were negotiating to play there. They came to watch a game, Australia against South Africa. One of them got fascinated. I explained the rules to him. He said it was a far better game than baseball. Action every minute. That doesn't happen in baseball.'

All the same, did he not think he was being a mite optimistic in earmarking the likes of Ireland and Holland for five-day status within ten years? 'No. We have a programme to raise standards. Australia "A" are going to Ireland and Scotland in a few weeks, with a strong team. We want them to get on TV, to promote the game. India "A" are going to Denmark and Holland. Pakistan are going there next year. Firstly, we want more teams in the World Cup. Secondly, Bangladesh will soon be the tenth Test team, and I'd like to get to twelve within the next five to ten years. I don't think that will compromise standards. New Zealand took nearly twenty-five years to win their first Test.

'Fortunately, the full member countries of the ICC, over the last couple of years, have become very supportive. They're bending over backwards to help the associate members raise their standards. New Zealand cricket's not a goldmine but they invited Bangladesh for a tour that cost them 40,000 quid. That type of gesture is now happening.'

The change of mood, he attests, dates back to the fractious ICC meeting of 1996. 'There was nearly a bust-up. Very ugly gathering. It was related to the presidency of the ICC. Dalmiya *v* Malcolm Gray of Australia. People were going round saying things like, "I'm not going to vote for your bloke". We [South Africa] blocked the vote. It was the cleverest thing we could have done for the future of world cricket. But there was a lot of aggro. The Australians were very unhappy we didn't vote for Gray. Said we had short memories. It was the cleverest thing we could have done because it resulted in a change of constitution, thanks mainly to Sir John Anderson [chairman of New Zealand cricket's governing body]. A very smart man. Got everyone together.'

Happily, the spluttering that greeted the accession of the ICC's first elected president, Jagmohan Dalmiya – who had caused no end of a stink with his proposal to ban draws in Tests – seems to have abated. Ali nods approvingly. As well he might. The pair met when Dalmiya, a prosperous Calcutta businessman, was secretary of the Indian Cricket Board. Armed with sufficient charms to strike up instant rapports with complete strangers, Ali made an exceedingly favourable impression, convincing Dalmiya to propose South Africa's readmission to the international brotherhood.

'Dalmiya's been good. He's part of the family now. He hasn't gone out to shout the odds. There's been a consensus of thought. And Australia will have the next president. We mustn't take it for granted that our future's secure. We're addressing the problems, working together. The type of administrators I'm seeing now are far better than they were ten years ago. The Australians have got an excellent chairman, Denis Rogers. Warm, sensible man. People on the subcontinent like him. There's Sir John Anderson – terrific man, a real salesman. Pakistan have Majid Khan, an honest, straight man. Sri Lanka have got Arjuna Ranatunga's brother. Came to South Africa for two weeks recently. Very good. Very strong. Everyone's bending over backwards to do the right thing.' And long – as the actress doubtless said to the bishop – may they bend.

AGITATION CREEPS IN just once. When I echo the consensus view that that week's ICC meeting had failed to uproot enough trees, not least with respect to the much-trumpeted – not to say much-belated – world championship. No other major sport has endured remotely so long without a legitimate barometer of its best. 'What didn't come out that should have come out,' Ali insists, exasperation plain, 'is that there's now a unanimous agreement to have reciprocal tours over a span of four to five years. England haven't toured Pakistan for what, eleven years! Everyone will play everyone else home and away during that span. With a minimum of three Tests per series. Every series will be for the world championship. Every Test will have value. It's just around the corner. So I don't know why everybody's saying nothing's happening.'

In the interests of logistics and harmony, are England and Australia truly prepared to cut their home–away cycle to twice a decade. 'Well … England, yes. Australia? Not great about that [idea]. But we're nearly there. We mustn't disturb traditional rivalries. We [South Africa] have a couple of commitments, like Australia back-to-back every four years, but we're happy to make it every five.'

And yes, glory be, he can also see the sense in awarding extra points for away wins. 'The point is, a one-off championship is not practical; a league is the only way. And we've established that. But I did not see one positive article on the meeting. To me, *that* was the positive. It'll be forthcoming in the next six months.' After 121 years, he might reasonably ask, what, pray, is six months?

'JONTY, JONTY'. The palatial dining-room at The Waldorf echoes to another Ali summons. Another trim green blazer looms into view. Jonty Rhodes (aka the aforementioned 'number six') comes over to the table, a spunky forty-seven not out overnight, fresh from writing the first chapter of South Africa's fightback at Lord's and en route to a matchwinning century. He seems extraordinarily sheepish, and apologises profusely. There had been times yesterday, he blushingly admits, when he 'got a bit carried away'. His team may have been on the rack but there he was, playing all those extravagant shots. The shame of it all. Ali's smile is kindly but distracted.

'Jonty, Jonty, I'd like you to go to Ireland next year, for a month,' he declaims in a tone that strongly suggests Jonty would be doing him the biggest personal favour since Zeus asked Hercules to clean up Athens. 'Steve Waugh's out there this August. You'll have a great time. They'll look after you extremely well. Help promote the game. I'll write back and tell them I've offered it to you.'

Vito Corleone, I can exclusively reveal, is alive and well and living in Johannesburg.

Chapter 8:
The Umpire's Tale

'If the bowler is the hired labourer
of the game, the umpire is indeed
the "Aunt Sally". He stands to be
criticised and maligned, the object of
the wordly projections of disappointed
batsmen, bowlers, and crowds who
always seem to know that [he] is a
hopeless, incapable fellow.'

Fred Root, *A Cricket Pro's Lot*, 1937

COUNTY Ground, Taunton, first Sunday in September. No lights, granted, but oodles of Uncle Rupert's super-duper cameras and, grizzly clouds permitting, action aplenty. Somerset (maroon-and-white) are preparing to take on Worcestershire (green-and-white) in the soon-to-be-deceased forty-over AXA League, a place in the First Division of next year's fifty-over as-yet unsponsored National League up for grabs.

Already the stands are thickening with pasty-packing picnickers. The cameraman below the press box is resplendent in ponytail and Reeboks. A car alarm warbles interminably. A small herd of even smaller boys clusters around Sky Sports' most famous summariser, Ian Botham, once and future king of these parts. As he proceeds towards the Ian Botham Stand, the Lord of the Lads appears to be thickening, too, mostly around the waist. Could this besuited, short-haired gent truly be the Hercules of Headingley? He looks discernibly shorter. Une trompe d'oeuil? Probably. Then again, once a warrior sheaths his sword, how can he but diminish?

John Harris is back at his former county and spiritual home. His grandfather, Harry Fernie, under whose roof he spent most of his childhood, was head groundsman here for quarter of a century. Residing in the club museum are two of the shoes that shod those trusty, uncomplaining steeds Harry employed to pull the roller. His grandson looks just a teensy bit self-conscious as he dons his powder-blue grocer's jacket. Adjusting his broad-brimmed sunhat, he picks up a pair of custard-yellow bails and begins to squeeze them. Perhaps he fancies his chances of filling Bogart's shoes as Captain Queeg in a remake of *The Caine Mutiny*? These fluorescent flannels are all very well for the players, but why couldn't they have got somebody with at least a sliver of taste to design the umpires' apparel? The Emmanuels would have fashioned something eye-catching but fetching. Better still, why not rope in that Paul Smith fella? He makes such swishy suits.

A blazered emissary from the England and Wales Cricket Board sidles over to ask John whether he would mind awfully if the game began at one o'clock sharp instead of five past? Botham and his chums will be transmitting live from 3.30 and their producer wants to be certain that one innings is done and dusted by then. John shrugs. If his fellow ump, John Holder, has granted his assent – which he has – then why should he have any objections? Anything to please.

Later that afternoon, one experienced Somerset player confesses that his side have had 'a bit of a thing' about John ever since he gave Martin Crowe out legbefore a couple of times the best part of a decade ago. Memories are as long as they are one-eyed. Nothing new, there, then. As R.C. Robertson-Glasgow warranted half a century ago: 'He is but a weak-kneed cricketer who *in his heart* approves of the umpire's decisions.'

Pity the poor ump. Ever since Robert Fitzgerald observed in 1866 that they 'were, for the most part, old women', these purported little Hitlers in white/powder-blue jackets have been the butt of more dark mutterings and wordy projections than any other on-field participant in any other sporting endeavour. For sheer volume of sustained sneers and loathing they comfortably outdo their whistle-waving counterparts: soccer referees, after all have only to endure the abuse for three hours' tops per week. If the umpire's eyesight is not being queried, his hearing is. Or his numeracy. Or impartiality. Or parentage. How often is he named man of the match? How seldom do his ears so much as tingle to the tune of praise. Justifying his decision to join Kerry Packer's breakaway troupe in 1977, John Snow captured the antipathy more succinctly than most, telling the High Court, tongue only partially inside cheek: 'I have nightmares about having to become an umpire.' Whither respect?

'There was no mass appealing in my day,' insisted Alf Gover, almost convincingly. 'The umpires would have told us off.' In the intense (and intensely insecure) world of professional cricket at the fag-end of the millennium such fears have dissolved like so much Disprin: a headache relieved. The very essence of the job is now under assault. From the belated introduction of independent officials in Tests to the birth of the third umpire and referee, most of the worthiest major measures taken by the authorities over the past decade have focused on Fitzgerald's old biddies: accepting their frailties but eroding trust; helping but exposing. Since the game reluctantly opened the technological Pandora's Box it has been forced to confront Medusa herself. Hell, there are even plans afoot to install an electronic detector (*à la* tennis) to spare any further fretting about no-balls. In the age of replays and reverse angles, steadicams and stump microphones, whither autonomy? And Dickie Bird, just to cap it all, is about to hang up his light meter. Bang goes the sex appeal.

'UMPIRING AT THE top now is full of comedians and gimmicks.' That was the parting shot of that plain-speaking Australian Cec Pepper, upon retiring from the first-class list in 1980. John Harris signed on three years later and has been a staple ever since. During those sixteen summers his branch of the game has witnessed change of a magnitude and significance that dwarfs the upheavals elsewhere. He appears to be coping well enough. A West Countryman through and through (despite a brief sojourn with his mother in south London), he is a gentle, unassuming, laid-back sort – Devon Man incarnate. His colleagues, indeed, dubbed him 'the Devon Gentleman'. Not for him the swanky stages and plush hotels, the Tests and Lord's finals, the Heathrows and the Jumbos. His beat has always been Fringe theatres and chummy B&Bs. Granted, he was forgivably aggrieved at being overlooked for the ultimate prize after spending seven years on the Test stand-by panel, but at sixty-two he can look back with pride on a turbulent trade plied ably and amiably. And, better still, unobtrusively. Which is just how he would have wished it. A comedian he most assuredly is not. Nor is he overly fond of gimmicks.

On days like this, does he feel duty-bound to supplement the razzmatazz with his own pizzazz? Cue extremely pregnant pause. He must choose his words with care. He is, after all, employed directly by the ECB and still has more than two years of his contract to run. He can't very well bite the hand that feeds so well (£20,000-plus for a season's work). Then again, a nibble can't hurt, can it? 'Well, we do get on with the job. We run around a lot, which is why we wear lighter shoes. The crowds give us a bit of stick because of the wides – they always think there's one when we probably don't. Or vice versa. I just give them a look, they have a laugh about it and off we go again. I've never been a lover of coloured clothing, except for under lights. If it works well then, perfect. Other than that I'm an old-fashioned person. I think about the white all the time.'

Barring that erstwhile PC Plod and fraud squadster Nigel Plews (who once compared his second career to being in a witness box – 'a very lonely place'), John is considerably lighter on first-class playing experience than his two dozen colleagues. Half a dozen of them, indeed, have played for their country. A useful leg-spinner in his youth, John also flew the flag, albeit only at schools level, whereupon Arthur Wellard, then Somerset's senior pro, advised him that he had 'the action to be a pace bowler' and ordered him to mend his ways that very day. Graduating to the Somerset first XI at sixteen as a briskish seamer capable of presenting an acceptably straight bat, John learned the ropes alongside the likes of Harold Gimblett and Colin McCool, Maurice Tremlett and Bertie Buse, the only man unfortunate enough to have his benefit match finish in a day. In 1954, National Service intervened.

'I had two years in the army and enjoyed it, played for them against everybody except the RAF and Navy – an officer took my place in those games – and found time to turn out for York Cricket Club. I learned a lot and nearly stayed, but I really wanted to give cricket another shot. I was still on Somerset's books, after all. I can remember coming back in 1956 and Bill Andrews, the coach, who I never got on well with, telling me I had to have a trial. I was a bit peeved but I went into the nets and all of a sudden Brian Langford and some of the other guys I knew started bowling wide outside my off-stump, giving me the opportunity to play my cover drive, which, being left-handed, I could play as well as anyone. They helped me through. Brilliant.'

In all there were 19 wickets at 32.57 in fifteen first-class appearances, most memorably a caught-and-bowled to remove the Demon Barber of Barbados himself, Everton Weekes (even if he did already have a double-hundred in the bank). John's aspirations, however, were brusquely squashed by a 'nasty' blow on the elbow from Middlesex's Alan Moss at Lord's. 'I had treatment but no X-ray. The first ball I bowled here afterwards cleared Harold Stephenson, our keeper, standing back. At that point it didn't actually hurt – I just thought I'd lost it. Next ball it did hurt. Very painful. Later on we found out that the joint had cracked either side. I still had another year to go on my contract but I knew I was struggling.'

In a sport that demands more of its officials than any other – including degrees in geometry, applied statistics and clairvoyance – overcoming such insubstantial grooming is not to be sniffed at. Having felt the full brunt of disappointment at an early age, John discovered something equally valuable: equanimity. His combination of tact and firmness, moreover, gained such pandemic respect among his *confrères* that he spent five years as chairman of their trade union, the Professional Umpires' Association (Barrie Meyer emphasised the ups and downs; Dickie Bird did the prodding and recommending). Negotiating patiently, skilfully and, ultimately, successfully, he helped secure salary rises and, more significantly, change in what had long been perceived as a grossly unfair marking system. That he has commanded such respect while suffering from 'blinding' migraines that render it quite impossible for him to function in public, is no less of an achievement.

The pleasure, quite plainly, easily outweighs the pain. 'I was very lucky to get into umpiring. It's the nearest I could get to the game. You can't have a better seat in the house than that. It's a thrill to watch these great players. The way Lara changes his mind before settling on a shot is incredible. Gave him lbw to complete his only pair to date. The player I've most enjoyed as an umpire was Graham Dilley [England fast bowler of the Eighties, one of the Headingley heroes with the bat in '81]. Lovely run-up, nice action, everything went through smoothly. Loved watching him. Viv [Richards] was good to watch when on song but you were always scared he was going to hit it straight!'

Has he ever experienced any bad shows of dissent? 'There's certainly no examples I can think of. Sure, players go off, eff a bit, show you their bat if you've given them lbw. Bill Alley used to tell me how he'd give people out and they wouldn't speak to him for the rest of the day. So next time he was umpiring them he'd go up and say, "Hear you're not speaking to me today coz I gave you out last time". They soon came round.'

'I try to make my point in a nice way,' he told David Foot in a 1997 interview for the *Western Daily Press* (in the Where Are They Now? Slot …). 'And that is how it stays until someone attempts to take advantage. Sledging does still go on. It was noticeable at the start of last season that the conduct of certain players was much improved. The riot act had been read to all of them on the question of discipline. Unfortunately, as the season went on, with more at stake, some aspects got back to normal. We have to accept that it isn't the game it used to be. There is need to have quiet words on the field with certain people and then see them again later.'

Does he still have a jar with the players? 'On occasion, but nowadays, with the breathalyser, most of them are in their cars and gone soon after the close. They also go home to their families more. A drink after the close used to be part of the game. I used to listen to the old umpires talk about their playing days, who they rated. It was very interesting but it doesn't happen much now. But you still form relationships, with players, other umpires, lovers of the game. It's just wonderful. As I came off at Lord's one day recently I saw three members of the Coventry and North Warwickshire club and we had a laugh and a joke. "What are you doing here?" I asked them. "We've come to watch you," said one. People coming to watch you at Lord's? Can't be bad.'

LEATHER AND WILLOW. John has tasted, consumed, smelled and breathed them ever since, at a painfully early age, his parents' divorce sent him to live with his grandparents ('just over the bridge there – Quantock it was called, third house down'). Grandad's love of the soil was duly transmitted.

'I'd have been about ten when I first came here, in '46, playing hooky from school. All the gatemen knew me. They waved me through and pointed out where grandad was, so I knew where to stand where he couldn't see me. Whenever he moved, I moved. He never saw me until after school was out. When I joined the staff as a teenager I used to help out – cleaning the bats, whitening the pads, polishing the brass taps in the first team's dressing-room. It was the only way you could get anywhere near there.'

Hence those plans to trace grandad's footsteps. 'I love groundwork. It's so rewarding to see green grass cut nicely, pitches nice and white, people saying it was a good pitch. I've got more feeling for groundwork than umpiring, truth be told. I disagree with groundsmen today because they all want to get rid of worms. I've always been a worm man. They help the water get away, get air down. They mix the soil so you don't get much layering. I've always felt it was wrong bringing in soils from all over the country. At Taunton, if we had anything other than local soil, it was Nottingham Marl – and it was just a dusting, not a layer. We'd get the soil in the shape of bricks then crush it up with the big roller in the stables. Then a lot of soil started coming through from Devon when the motorway began to go through. One summer when my grandad was groundsman we had a pony to pull the roller: I gave the club museum two of its shoes. But grandad kept four big boots from the horses he used to pull it. He passed them down to me, and I shall pass them down to Tim, my youngest son.'

Upon leaving Somerset John coached for a spell at Framlingham public school, representing Suffolk and Devon in the Minor Counties championship when duties permitted, then took over as head groundsman at St Edmund's School in Canterbury before moving on to fulfil the same role at Sidmouth.

'I did ten years there. Put a lot into it. My first marriage certainly suffered. I did have the opportunity to do the job here, at Taunton, when Don Price left in the early Seventies, but my wife wasn't very keen: she was very happy in Sidmouth. And there's no way I'd commute back from Bath or Weston-super-Mare with all the traffic around Bridgewater and what have you. So I went to Exeter, to take over the Devon county ground. I was also asked whether I fancied going to Old Trafford but I realised that I'd probably have been jumping in too deep, and also that my wife didn't want to go to Manchester. Nor did I, really. Too much of a West Countryman. But I still wanted something better, more money.'

That grounding in groundsmanship has been an undoubted boon, and not merely because John has served fifteen consecutive years as the umpires' representative on the TCCB/ECB Pitches Committee (he is still pitch inspector for the Devon League and would dearly love to continue on the committee once he has counted his last pebble). Being able to talk to groundsmen in their own language, and comprehending the ins and outs of preparation and covering better than most, means he is more able to tell whether a pitch is likely to be playable, or what you should do, and when. Or whether the curators are slinging the lead, putting their precious square before players and public. Although he is more inclined to blame impetuous strokes and grotty techniques for the woeful collapses that littered the 1998 county championship, and even though only one club, Northamptonshire, was hauled before the ECB beaks and deducted 25 points for preparing an unfit surface, the state of pitches remains a cause for grave concern.

'There's just not enough bounce. It makes you wonder whether the soil is dying. We've a good crop of groundsmen but the money dried up a bit a few years ago and some of the younger ones were tempted elsewhere.' He has also noted a greater pressure to grin and bear the elements. 'Sponsorship has made a difference. Company directors come with their guests, the sun's out and they want to see play. Years ago people would accept the interruptions more willingly.'

Today was more like the old days. Somerset had lost nearly half the side in fewer than half their alotted overs when drizzle begat mini-deluge. And that, apart from one blink-or-you'll-miss-it passage, proved to be that. During tea, shortly after a presentation had been made in the indoor school to Eric Hill, the kindly septuagenarian whose last reporting stint was about to meet a watery end, John was confronted in the members' bar by an extremely small boy. When, he insisted on knowing, would play resume? The regretful smile and pursed lips were answer enough; offical confirmation followed a few minutes later. There were no remonstrations, no cracks or digs. Then again, with one game left, two points per side for an abandonment was infinitely preferable to losing four to a close rival. For the home team, given the state of the contest, a no-result was actually quite a bit of a result.

What of the pitch? The eyebrows shrug. 'Well, ideally what you want for a one-day match is average to above-average pace, not turning. People want to see runs. I've just had a pitch – I won't tell you where – for a Sunday League game which we marked poor. It had already been used for four days of a championship match. We warned them beforehand but they still used it. This one is average, below. It turned – whew! We don't want to see that really. If Somerset had been in the field it would have been different, because they've got Andy Caddick, so the ball would have run through quicker. Some groundsmen get good pace marks because, nine times out of ten, they work for clubs with a good pace attack. It's all so unfair really.'

QUALIFYING AS AN umpire, I read out from an article in *The Guardian*, currently requires aspirants to pass a brace of written exams as well as an oral test; unless, that is, you have played the game at first-class level. 'Until now,' as Graham Bullock, administration manager of the Association of Cricket Umpires and Scorers, recently pointed out, 'ninety-nine per cent of the people going on to the first-class list have been retired players'. The exam issue, however, is currently a hottish potato: there is a growing conviction that some form of written or verbal evidence of a candidate's command of theory should be mandatory. Happily, this is b eing phased in. John concurs. 'It has always been felt that if you'd played professionally then an exam wasn't necessary, as in my case, especially at Minor Counties level, although I'd always urge any would-be umpire to take it.'

Juggling job and ambition was no easy matter. 'At first I carried on playing at weekends [one red-letter season for Sidmouth yielded 2356 runs and one hundred wickets making him the first player to do the 'double' for the club] and umpired other club games in midweek. Sometimes I'd leave the ground at Exeter while the game was going on, and go and umpire somewhere, but I didn't do that very often because I knew I'd get into trouble if I wasn't back in Exeter for the change of innings. If I was covered I was all right.

'Devon recommended me to the Minors. The Dorset skipper had a few words too: little chappie, opened for Hants, went to Charterhouse as coach … Anyway, next thing I knew I was on the reserve list. I graduated to the main list and then applied to Lord's. Donald Carr was the Test and County Cricket Board's chief executive then. He sent me back a letter every year for a few years, saying "sorry,

Gentleman's relish… John enjoys a quip from South Africa's doughty all-rounder Brian McMillan, Trent Bridge 1998 (*John Harris Collection*)

Above: Happiness is a fully-functioning biro… Byron Denning, Hove, July 1998 (*Graham Goldwater*)

Left: Different plane… Byron with Viv Richards, 1993: 'We flew in two six-seater aircraft from Swansea to Colwyn Bay. Personnel were carefully divided, so as least valuable, I sat next to Viv.' (*Byron Denning Collection*)

Right: Heard that one before… Byron and his wife Olwen, who has ferried him to all Glamorgan's away matches since his heart attack, together in the 'Shed' at Sophia Gardens for the last time before the stand was pulled down, September 1998 (*Graham Goldwater*)

Above: Royal flush… Huw Morris, the Glamorgan captain, tells Prince Charles about the time Byron (*fourth from left*) dared to introduce Waqar Younis as 'Waqar Hussain' (*Byron Denning Collection*)

Left: Number-crunchers… Byron with the Nottinghamshire scorer, Len Beaumont, at Trent Bridge (*Byron Denning Collection*)

Below: Once in a generation… Byron clutches the county championship trophy at Taunton, 1997: Glamorgan's first such title since 1969 and only their third since they graduated to the first-class ranks in 1921 (*Byron Denning Collection*)

Game over… Glamorgan and Somerset players leave the field at the end of the last match of the season while Byron announces that the hosts have achieved their biggest-ever margin of victory in terms of runs – Cardiff, September 1998 (*Graham Goldwater*)

The precious few… spectators find other diversions after the early finish, Cardiff, September 1998 (*Graham Goldwater*)

your application has not been accepted" etc. I think they looked at me and thought, well, there are players coming out of the game without a job – and I had one. I thought I'd missed the boat.'

The circumstances of his finally getting on board remain engraved on the retina in more ways than one. 'Suddenly, out of the blue, I had a call at home from Brian Langley, the TCCB assistant secretary: I was on the full list. Trouble was, I'd just had a horrendous migraine when the phone rang. I'd been lying down with the curtains drawn. For three weeks I wasn't sure whether I'd dreamt it!

'Earlier that day I'd gone into the shed at Exeter and sat in the dark to try and get rid of it. I'd tried it three times that day but still couldn't shake it off. Felt sick, pins and needles in my arms, blind. I always go blind. I can only see light and dark. I've had a few since I've been on the circuit, including one at Chelmsford last week. I saw the old flashlights and went straight away. I looked up for the sixth ball of the over and I could only see one pad. Barrie Leadbeater was the other umpire, so I went up to him, and then the fielding captain, and said, "Sorry, got a migraine, gotta go". They understand, but it's a nuisance, a pain. Although there's always a replacement on hand, he can only stand at square leg, so my mate has to do twice as much work, so you try and hurry back. At Chelmsford I went straight into the shower area and sat in a chair for half an hour until lunch. Something to eat helped and I was back in the afternoon.

'The worst such episode was with Alan Whitehead at Portsmouth two years back. Second morning and I told him I was having one. He understands because his daughter also suffers from migraines. There was no way I could stand. He had to do both ends all day. The most I've ever done on my own is forty minutes! It's hard work.'

John paid his dues on the reserve list, spending the summers of 1981 and 1982 flexing his forefinger in university and second XI bouts. 'It was a big jump from the Minors to first-class. Neil Williams had just started with Middlesex and I took his first ball. Looked up to see him bowl and the ball was already in the wicketkeeper's gloves! Hullo, I thought. I've got to work a bit harder here. I was standing with Lloyd Budd, an ex-copper. He was very helpful. "Don't worry son," he said, "when I leave you'll get my place." Which is effectively what happened. One day Brian Langley asked what I was doing that winter. "I've got my job at Exeter," I told him. "Well," he said, "you won't earn much doing this – we've just given the umpires a pay rise, to 9000." Which was *three times* what the Exeter job was worth.' Even now he looks as if he needs to pinch himself.

Others, particularly those at the sharper and more remunerative end, have been known to be a tad less grateful. Take another copper-turned-umpire, Tom Brooks. When I bumped into him behind the Warner Stand at the 1997 Lord's Test, the statuesque Australian remarked, with much melancholy, how leaving the increasingly fractious international arena two decades earlier was one of the most sensible things he ever did. Having been obliged to take a front-row seat for some of the most unpleasant Tests ever held, it was hard to blame him. 'By the time Robin Baillache and I walked into the hotel in Sydney at the end of the [1974–75 Ashes] series, I found myself turning to him and saying, "Thank God – I can't wait to finish."' Upon bidding his final adieu after the 1978–79 Ashes rubber, Brooks amplified the point: 'I couldn't see why I should stand there and have players looking at me as if I were a leper.' One senses a modicum of relief when John notes that the most high-profile games of his career were NatWest Trophy and Benson and Hedges Cup semi-finals.

Did he glean any worthwhile advice? 'Just after I got on the list I bumped into Len Coldwell, the old Worcestershire and England fast bowler, whom I'd known from his days at Somerset. "Any tips?" I asked him. "Just give yourself time before you make any decisions," he said. "As a player I shout and expect the umpire's finger to go straight up. Give yourself time." So I started to say, "That's … out" or "That's … not out". During that pause I'm mentally replaying it.'

Had he ever suffered from premature ejaculation? Or, to put it more discreetly, had his trigger finger ever been so itchy it acted independently? 'Once, a couple of seasons ago. They all went up for an lbw appeal and I brought my right hand all the way round – I usually have both behind my back – then realised I'd decided to give it not out. So, as the bowler has his back to me running down the pitch in celebration – having seen my initial reaction – I carried my hand right round to my pocket, took out my notebook and pretended I needed to check something.' The reaction of the thwarted bowler went unrecorded.

The most unusual incident? No contest: Ed Giddins and the Amazing Ambidextrous Delivery, even if it did have the entirely predictable effect of turning sleight of hand into controversy. 'I was standing at Leicester for the championship match against Sussex and I thought Ed was letting the ball go early, as his right arm was going through the action. It turned out that he was bowling it with his left hand! During the interval somebody asked me whether I'd no-ball a bowler for changing hands. "Uh oh," I thought. "What's going on here?" Next time he bowled I noticed the sunlight on the ball on its way down even though he had yet to go through his action, so I no-balled him. Normally, if you call a no-ball from square leg, because it's an illegal delivery, everyone looks at you. So I stick my hand out and I'm thinking, "Ooh er, all hell's going to be let loose now". But nothing happened. The ball was thrown back to Giddins and he got on with it. Nobody said a word. None of the press mentioned it either, until Martin Searby turned up the next morning to ask what had happened. And that's how the rumour started about Ed being a chucker. I can't remember ever reporting anyone's action.' So now we know.

Does he have any tricks to maintain concentration? 'No, no,' he chuckles. 'I think I slipped up very early – missed two stumpings because my eyes and my mind had wandered. But I was lucky: I got 'em right! You keep concentrating if you're relaxed physically, so you stand up there but you sit back. Head's got to be still.'

Every April, John and his colleagues undergo a full medical, including, for some, a thorough ear syringe. 'I can read the bottom line of the chart now,' he quips with a dash of blackish irony: last winter he had a cataract removed from his right eye. 'The surgeon said that there had been a lot of damage from an old injury – when I was 10 an eating fork had been stuck in my eye. I knew I'd have to have something done over the next five years but suddenly it all went wrong. I saw a specialist straight away, on a Wednesday; had the operation the next Tuesday. They rebuilt the whole of the area behind the eye. Magic.

'That's helped me this year. I think knowing I had only three years left has made me more relaxed. I do the job more without thinking about it. I worry less about the marks. People always say that we shouldn't worry about the marks, that the board'll never get rid of us, but they've got rid of certain umpires if their marks have been consistently low.'

What, then, of H.D. Bird Esq.? His marks, particularly in the twilight years of his Test career, could hardly be described as consistently high. 'What can I say? Dickie's been a good person, put umpiring on the map. His marks might well have been low on a few occasions, but the players all rate him. Perhaps some captains haven't but that's how it goes.

'My marks were very consistent for the first ten years then I dropped ten places in one season – and I've hovered there ever since. I did better last year, and I can honestly say I've never finished bottom. But honestly, from top to twenty-fifth or whatever, the difference is never that great. On the full list we're not given marks anymore. We used to be marked one to five, which enabled you to catch up quicker than when it was one to ten, which is now the case with the reserve umpires. In our case, as from this year, the captains fill in an assessment form halfway through the season and again at the end, giving a general overview, which is a definite plus. The idea is to make them think a bit more before delivering their verdict. Not sure what we'll talk about at our meetings now. Having the captains assess halfway through the season and at the end, rather than after every match, as is happening this season, is a definite plus. Not sure what we'll talk about at our meetings now.'

How objective can captains be? 'I have known several first-class umpires,' noted Fred Root, that erudite England seamer of the inter-war era, in his seminal autobiography *A Cricket Pro's Lot*, 'who have been exceedingly worried when it has fallen to their lot in successive innings to give decisions against captains. One famous umpire gave one of our popular county captains out lbw to me, and when the batsman was making his way pavilionwards, turned to me and said, "I do wish he would keep his legs out."'

Surely a losing skipper is more inclined to vent his spleen? 'Until this season, certainly, the captains had too much of an influence. Some, by their nature or their personality, might not get on with a certain umpire and may mark accordingly. Years ago, when every championship match was played over three days, one captain always marked satisfactory or down. If you had him for five or six matches there was no way you were going to finish anywhere near the top. No way. But then you might get another who marked high. Swings and roundabouts. If you had all the captains during the course of a season you'd get a fair reflection, but sadly you don't.'

Can he recall any stinkers? 'I don't think I've ever come home thinking I'd had an awful game. I have gone home and said to myself, "Well, I got that lbw wrong". If you give someone lbw and he got a nick on it, he might pop round at the end of the day and say, "Hey John, I got a nick on that". But I don't think I've ever gone away thinking I had a *horrendous* time. I do feel bad if I've made a bad decision because you do have a big responsibility for people's careers, but you can only do it as you see it. The number of playing conditions that have come in has certainly made the job harder. It's not just the Laws we need to know anymore. Every time a playing condition comes in the players try to work a way round it. It's human nature. So we have to have another playing condition to stop that. Then you get a bouncer restriction.'

Speaking of which, would it be terribly unreasonable to infer that he and his colleagues were a mite too lenient on intimidatory bowling, that they lacked the courage to enforce the full wrath of Law 42.8 (d) and ban players if they crossed that ill-defined line? That, in short, it was their shortcomings that made the restriction necessary? 'I've read that, but I honestly think we were starting to get it right when we had the change to two per over. The West Indies certainly used the short ball in a way we never did. We saw it as a surprise. When they brought the law in I remember speaking to Courtney Walsh about too many short-pitched deliveries. He gave it to me straight, saying, "You just tell me when it's one for the over, man." Great man, Courtney.'

AND SO TO the day's most scalding potato. To tolerate human error or not to tolerate human error? Peter Willey, one of the handsomely-paid members of the ICC International Panel, and as such a man whose errors are exposed with rather more ruthless regularity than John's, had been raising hackles. Questioned after the ICC's umpires conference, he had asserted, semi-seriously, that the haste with which technology was now being embraced might make it advisable for the game to henceforth confine his breed to the role of pebble-counters and sweater-holders. A rash of umpiring errors in the Test series against South Africa had brought matters to a foaming head. The crux, for the more thoughtful Luddites, is that where the camera sometimes lies, flesh and blood merely err. Wherever one stands, the bottom line is that the profession has reached a watershed. Late in the day as it is for him, does John feel threatened?

'The cameras have certainly made things difficult for us,' he demurs. 'I felt at first, because we couldn't consult them ourselves, that they weren't going to help us, but I think they've proved that most umpires get most things right. But now we've got this slow-slow-motion, and this circle that homes in on the ball, affording a view we couldn't possibly hope to have.' Lengthy pause. 'I just ...' Even lengthier pause. 'I suppose it's exciting for the crowd to see you motion for the replay then wait for that red or green light to come on.

'I made a mistake at Canterbury recently. I didn't consult the third umpire. I thought a stumping was well out. When I came off, Graham Burgess, the third umpire, came up and said, "Do you want to know about that stumping?" Chris Balderstone, the other umpire, turned to him and asked: "Why? That was out wasn't it?" "Well, no," said Burgess. So you sit down, absolutely amazed. "He never got back," I said. "No, he never left," said Burgess. And that's even worse. Sky did so many frames they established that he never left his crease until after the stumps were broken. Since then I've said, right, I'm going to the camera every time there's a line decision. Beefy [Botham] was commentating that day and said it was one occasion when you *had* to consult the third umpire; now I agree. But it looked *so* out.

'One big drawback with the cameras being at midwicket is that I feel I don't really want to get into the right position to judge a run-out because nine times out of ten I'll block the camera. Fortunately, since I'm normally operating without them, you do what should be second nature.'

So what is it to be? Kitchen sink or nothing? Cameras for all or none? 'That's a very difficult question,' he says, weaving skilfully, just as he did when he boxed in his youth (for a dare, he once donned the gloves at a fairground booth and was paid for his considerable pains). 'When they first brought TV replays in for line decisions, Barry Meyer – a great friend of mine and the umpire I most respect because he had so much commonsense, made you feel so comfortable when you stood with him – was quite pleased: he'd always struggled with run-outs. He'd always ask people: "What do you watch? The line? The bat? Both?" He couldn't seem to get it quite right. When we discussed the stump camera at our umpires' meeting we said we didn't want it. So we didn't have it in the first year. Then the board brought it in. So we all thought, where's it going to end? Anyway, if you're going to go the whole hog you're going to need a lot of umpires. Helluva big expense.'

But surely, in the interests of getting it right, with so much at stake, such a move should be regarded as an investment? Another deft weave. 'The time will come when every ground has its own cameras, like Lord's has. I don't know if it's a good thing or not. I think we need help because players don't walk anymore. Or few do. Dear old "Bluey" Bairstow [the former Yorkshire captain who'd died at his own hand a few months previously] used to. And Craig White, another Yorkie, walked in a one-day match a year or so ago, which was wonderful, and I thanked him for it, but when I was playing you could actually name five players who *didn't* walk. The money's changed things, of course. I just wish we could go back to being the men in the middle doing a job. But I don't think that's ever going to happen.'

BESIDES, WHY DWELL on the bad when the good has been so plentiful? 'Sylvester Clarke was one of the best fast bowlers I've ever seen. Although there was this little "nick" noise, like a joint, when he bowled his really quick one, I wouldn't like to say he was a chucker. I'll tell you a funny story about him, though. Oval, local derby, Surrey versus Middlesex, he runs in and bowls a fast bouncer to Norman Cowans, the Middlesex number eleven. Norman went to ground, crawled round the stumps, I called "no-ball" and walked about halfway down the pitch. Clarkie just stood there looking at me. Then Ian Greig, the Surrey captain, came running up to me saying, "What's that for John?" So I told him: "Number eleven – I don't think he knows what end to hold." So now Clarkie's leaning beside the stumps. As I turned round and walked back, he's saying, "It's a girl's game – this is a girl's game". So I'm thinking, be strong John, be strong. "Go on, Clarkie," I said. "You get back and bowl."

'Next ball was a nice gentle half-volley and Cowans smeared it for four. Clarkie turned to me and said, "Is that all right?" "Clarkie," I said, "You don't have to be like this. You're a better bowler than that. You don't have to bowl bouncers at a number eleven." Next ball was another soft one: Cowans missed, I think. Then the next one ripped all three stumps out. As we walked off, me feeling pretty chuffed, happy that I'd stepped in at the right time, Clarkie's pointing at me, saying, "I'm gonna get you man, I'm gonna get you man." I saw him across the bar in the Tavern that night and we had a chat. I reiterated what I'd said earlier, that he was ferocious enough without having to bowl bouncers at someone like Cowans. "Well," he said, "he pinched one of my girls." I gulped. I could have had a war on my hands!'

At this, a grin the breadth of the Quantocks erupts across those ruddy features. The parting, we may rest assured, will be more sorrowful than sweet.

Chapter 9:
The Scorer's Tale

'There was a social prejudice
against the scorer, a descendant of
the baggage man.'

Vic Issacs, Hampshire scorer and statistician

BYRON DENNING clears his throat, checks the wording on the piece of paper by his computer and reaches for the public address microphone. 'Grahame Lloyd will be signing copies of Daffodil Days *in the club shop after the game,' he announces in that rich, sonorous baritone. 'Many thanks to everyone who has bought the book – hope you enjoyed it.'*

Twelve months on and the glow still lingers. The sight of Somerset batsmen trooping to and from the Sophia Gardens pavilion supplies a welcome dose of *déjà vu* at the end of a dismal summer. This time last year, after all, the Glamorgan players were painting Taunton a deep shade of red, county champions for the third time in the club's predominantly glitter-free history. It is hard to picture any other county inspiring a journalist to devote much space in a book about an historic season, if any, to the club scorer, but then how many other counties represent a nation? Lloyd's account of that euphoric September afternoon and the months that preceded it contains a chapter entitled The Thirteenth Man. Byron 'Dasher' Denning deserved nothing less.

Moments later, match and season are over. Even though Glamorgan have just pulled off their handsomest victory of all time in terms of runs – 298 – the jubilation, unsurprisingly, doesn't quite have the same intensity. Byron puts down his pen and addresses the crowd once more. 'Farewell to you all. Have a good winter and I hope you all come back again refreshed next summer.' Boys and dads stroll on to request monikers and pat backs. The players hug and high-five. Filing into the dressing-room they re-emerge in shorts and get stuck into a game of football. A trio of teenage girls approach a sweaty Matthew Maynard: would he mind awfully posing for a photo? Outside the ground, a billboard carries a puff for a *Wales On Sunday* interview with the Glamorgan skipper ('You watch us next season'). A few picnickers stay rooted to their seats, riveted by Maynard the Dribble and James the Tackle. They've paid their money: let the entertainment continue.

Up in the portakabin that doubles as media centre and scorers' box, Byron removes another pen from the daffodil-crested pocket of his smart blue club blazer and fills in his ECB Scorer's Report (stamped 'confidential', naturally). He asks if I could wait a few more minutes: the *Western Mail* need his report of yesterday's rugger-buggery between Pontypool and UWIC. 'See you over there,' says David Oldam, Somerset's kindly, Friar Tuckish number-cruncher. 'Wee-eell,' hesitates Byron, apologetic but clearly distracted. 'I don't know. I've got to file my rugby. Grateful for your co-operation. Couple of senile old scorers together, eh?'

'Six brilliant wins but when we lose …' begins Oldam, trailing off as exasperation bites. 'No consistency.' In an interview with the *South Wales Echo* a couple of springs back Byron had pinpointed the most arduous part of the job: keeping his partiality in check. 'I get exhilarated when we win and depressed when we lose, and I know most of my mates in the box are exactly the same. But we try our best to maintain a professional dignity while we are working … but it's not easy.'

He proposes we chat in 'the shed', the antique wooden stand to the right of the portakabin, due to be pulled down during the winter as part of an extensive redevelopment programme. There we meet Olwen, aka Mrs Dasher, a cheery woman with a smile as soft as melting molasses. They are a rare team indeed. Ever since Byron's first heart attack a few years back, Olwen has accompanied him on assignments from North Yorkshire to Southampton, not only driving him everywhere but helping lug around all those scorebooks, yearbooks and interminable reams of rules, regulations and forms. On occasion she operates the scoreboard here. And no, she doesn't need to be reminded that one of those occasions was that sorry Saturday afternoon last June when Middlesex bowled her boyos out for 31 (the front page of the *Western Mail* sports section the following Monday was dominated by a snapshot of the all-revealing scoreboard at the end of the innings, Olwen clearly visible through the window directly under the figure '31'). 'Operating the board suits her well,' insists Byron. 'It's a job that entails watching very carefully and not being distracted, which is the way Olwen likes to watch her cricket.'

Here, quite patently, is no ordinary cricket widow. So, how did she feel about the job that had consumed her husband's summers since he took early retirement from teaching in 1984? 'I think the first season he did was a novelty really. Ooh, yes, follow Glamorgan around! After that, when spring came around, I started to realise he'd be gone all summer again. He was supposed to have *retired*. I think I got over the hump around the third season.'

'Gradually she got used to it,' grins Byron. 'Then I got my heart attack and she started accompanying me. There was a nurse following me around! But she's enjoyed it.'

'I *love* the game,' stresses Olwen. 'We used to come here when we were courting.'

'She used to come to the old Arms Park ground down the road. I don't think she saw a wicket taken or a run scored for about three seasons as she knitted or read. But she's grown to love the game and now she's an avid supporter. She used to score for Ebbw Vale when I umpired. She actually watches, too, doesn't talk like most of the other ladies.'

How did the opportunity to go on the road arise? 'I fell into it when Frank

Culverwell hung up his pencils. I'd been on the committee for fifteen years. The only decision I remember helping to take was whether to employ Javed Miandad or Winston Davis as our overseas player. I was one of the two out of twenty-four who voted for Winston. I'd never been much of a player. The only time I played for Cross Keys first XI was at Lydney every Cup Final weekend: nobody else wanted to play. But I always thought, right, if you can't play properly at least you could help administer it. Anything to be involved.

'The tales about Frank are legion. He perpetually had arguments with the scoreboard operators: they always thought they were right and he was wrong, and vice versa. He'd get very irate with reporters who came asking for bowling figures at the end of the day. His classic reply was: "Oh, I can't be bothered with that. They'll be in the paper in the mornin'."'

JAUNTY AND JOCULAR as he is for a seventy-year-old saddled with gout and a dicky ticker, Byron looks drained. Given that he has had to watch every ball of every over of every day of every match for the past five months, this is not entirely surprising. As a mere reporter – and you know how little *we* watch – I used to be staler than yesterday's toast come mid-July.

'I'm tired,' he confirms needlessly. 'When I started I thought, great, watching Glamorgan and getting paid for it (we got a £500 honorarium though I'd have done it for free). Gateway to heaven. But doing it for a whole season is one hell of a lot of concentration. I don't think people realise how demanding scoring is, particularly since the advent of computers means you're doing two jobs instead of one. I'm relieved the season is over but the way I look at it, throughout the season I'm looking forward to the rugby season and through the rugby season I'm looking forward to cricket. There's always a new season.'

'You do get a bit stale towards the end of a summer,' Olwen reminds him.

'Tired, tired. But at least tomorrow morning I won't have to get up at half-past seven.'

Olwen nods slowly, knowingly, drawing on expertise gathered through fourteen long winters. 'For the first week you say, "great, I'm out of it now" – and I know you enjoy the rugby reporting – but you soon miss it.'

As much as anything, he treasures the interaction with the players, the way they were willing to embrace a chap twice their age. 'We were travelling to Worcester once – Rodney Ontong driving, Alan Butcher in the passenger seat, me in the back. Just before we left Swansea the barmaid at the club there gave me this quiz book on pop music, so as to pass the time away, I played question master. The answer to one question was Chuck Berry. After I read it out they were humming and hawing, didn't really know. "I'll give you a hand," I said. "If this fellow was bowling he'd be no-balled by the square-leg umpire." So they stalled, then Butcher came out with a classic. "I know," he said, "Percy Thrower!" I think we swerved off the road at that point.'

Besides last season's glory-glorying and the Sunday League triumph five summers ago, Byron's other favourite cockle-warmer is a masterful Viv Richards century against Hampshire. 'Viv was great. Everyone wondered how he was going to be when he joined us. I think the players, whilst they appreciated him, were in awe. I've never been in awe of anybody. One time Matthew Maynard ran Viv out at Swansea and Viv came into the dressing-room – I only learned this afterwards – and was very angry, throwing his bat around. I had to come to the dressing-room for something and I said to him something to the effect of, "Here Viv, you were a bit unlucky there – you were both in but at the same end". I was joking of course. Alan Butcher looked at me as if I was mad. Talk about diving in where angels fear to tread. Viv took it in good heart. I suppose, to an extent, I may have alleviated the tension. Mind you, he could have clobbered me with his bat.'

IT WOULD NOT be unreasonable to suppose that a scorer must have some affinity for numbers. Without that boyish zeal for the way a row of figures can act as shorthand for the most fabulous facts imaginable, how can you handle the sheer repetition? Meet a proud exception. 'Never been interested in statistics. I keep an averages book, obviously. The players only ask to look when they're doing well; most of them are pretty on the ball. But I'm not a statistician; I'm a simple, plain scorer. I know the facts. Dr Hignell, the club statistician, supplies everything that's required. I leave that to my betters.'

All that said, there are at least two numbers embedded in his brain: 302 and 287. The former represents Wally Hammond's score at Newport on the first day's cricket Byron saw with his father in 1939 ('I can still recall Glamorgan's extra-cover repeatedly watching the ball pass him and making no real effort to dive; they didn't do that in those days, and no running after the ball – much too silly'). The latter was Emrys Davies' riposte. 'Still our highest score,' he declares resignedly. 'I didn't see that. Typical, eh?'

And of course there was that almighty explosion at the Arms Park a couple of decades later, when Jim McConnon walloped 28 runs off an over from Sussex's Ian Thomson. 'Six, four, four, six, four, four,' he recites as if chanting a mantra.

Given his illustrious forename, he had long fancied writing 'the odd ode': so stirred was he by McConnon's almighty swipe through a window of a flat in Westgate Street, he returned to Cross Keys and got scribbling. It was published in the *South Wales Echo*:

You've all heard of 'Jim and the buildings',
Of 'Take It From Here' radio fame
Have you heard of Glamorgan's Jimmy,
Who shines at a far different game?

Last week against Sussex at Cardiff,
His figures were five-fifty-four;
Then wielding the willow with power,
He put fifty-two on the score.

Twenty-eight runs came from one over,
Poor Thomson – he hadn't a clue
But even his south county colleagues
Said it was quite a 'Smart' thing to do.

But let's spare a thought for Miss Bradshaw,
Whose window was broken in twain –
We hope that it soon will be mended –
So that Jimmy can break it again!

(In case the reference eludes, the 'Smart' alludes to Cyril Smart, another Glamorgan slugger who plastered 32 off an over from Hampshire's Hill at Cardiff in 1935.)

There was also one number that appalled, and still does. You can find it easily enough in *Wisden*, in the Fastest Hundreds section, under 'contrived circumstances': twenty-one, the number of minutes Lancashire's Glen Chapple took to reach three figures against Glamorgan at Old Trafford in 1993 – to 'expedite a declaration', as the good book so quaintly puts it. The first-class game has never witnessed a speedier century, nor one more empty. Byron winced at each and every false, meaningless blow. 'Oh dear, that was horrendous. More so for Bill Davies, the Lancashire scorer, because he was operating the computer; the home scorer usually does. Oh, it was horrendous. I think there was a four off the first ball. The fielders were letting the ball go to the boundary, sometimes standing outside it. It was so-oo ludicrous. In the first over a wicket was taken and we suddenly realised there'd been seven balls as well: we'd missed a no-ball sign. Now in the first place, when fielders aren't fielding and every ball is a four or a six, entering this into a computer is not easy. By the end of the second over Bill just couldn't cope. He'd had to enter a wicket, add in a no-ball, and then the next over had gone for twenty. When Chapple did get to his century poor Bill was still trying to put the sixth over – I think it all lasted ten or twelve overs – into the laptop.

'The reporters wanted to know how many balls he'd faced, how long he'd been batting, but there was no way we could cope with anything but putting the runs into the book and then into the machine. I never want to be involved with anything like that again. It was completely farcical. Not only that, it was stressful, for Bill in particular. It was one of the reasons he retired, I believe.

'Concentration is especially difficult to maintain in situations like that, in what I term the "meaningless" third innings, where you know very well the side bowling isn't really trying to get the other side out. It'd be a lot easier if, at the end of the second innings, the side batting next decided how many runs they were going to score and we came back the following day at 2 p.m. The computer doesn't help, of course.'

AH, TECHNOLOGY. BANE of the scorer as well as the umpire. If not more so. Acquainting eighteen mostly sixty-somethings steeled in biro and paper with the intricacies of keyboard and microchip was always going to be a task of Sisyphean proportions. All the same, as the Duke of the Dot Ball himself, Bill 'Bearded Wonder' Frindall, underlined in the 1994 *Wisden*, the groundwork was considerably less assiduous than it might have been (even though Computer Newspaper Services had guaranteed the TCCB a cool £40,000 to instigate computerised scoring). 'On the face of it, the introduction of the computer was a logical development,' he wrote, 'perhaps even an inevitable one, utilising technology to improve the art of scoring and construct a potentially valuable database. However, a change of this magnitude needed to be conceived with infinite care and planning. Three things should have been considered essential: a pilot scheme to locate and eradicate the experimental system's inevitable blips; a comprehensive training programme; and the maintenance of a back-up system in the form of a manual scorebook. Lamentably, none of those three essentials was available to the county scorers when they reported for duty last April.'

In the annals of militancy, it scarce needs pointing out, scorers are roughly on a par with monks and cocker spaniels. On this occasion, however, the counters were up in arms and ready to march on Lord's. One complained about a thirteen-step manoeuvre to record a stumping off a wide: just the ticket when you're monitoring a one-day game. Hampshire's Vic Isaacs and Surrey's Michael Ayres were especially voluble; the beefs aired by the latter when I interviewed him for *The Independent* earned him a reprimand from the club (and may even have contributed, I fear, to his sacking at the end of term). Short runs and sundry unusual dismissals – such as handled the ball – were simply not recognised. Byron was equally unamused.

'We've *never* had adequate training; it's always been rushed. The software was often, well, poor. I can say that of this season, too. There are so many things that are faulty. For instance, if a run is scored on the last ball of an over it doesn't automatically appear on screen until you've closed that over. So you think you're one run short. Another idiotic thing: it won't accept any wicket falling off the first ball of an innings. You've got to fiddle around, enter a seven-ball over then come back and correct it. It's quite unbelievable. I don't want to say who designed the software; I don't want to be involved in a libel case. But it really has doubled our workload because we still fill in the scorebooks as well.

'The first time I was involved with one was at Derby. At lunch, Stan [Tracey, the home scorer] just couldn't operate anymore. So we ceased using the computer, rang the powers-that-be and just said we couldn't do it. We reverted to telephone and called the scores over every ten minutes. I'm not saying the computer isn't beneficial. Balls faced and the number of fours for each batsman are displayed on the screen; all the bowling figures are readily available. And now they've introduced archive material which will enable you to do the averages as well. That will presumably be helpful – *when* it works properly. You've also got one of those spider's webs, as I call them, recording where a batsman's shots go. And you can keep in touch with every match that's being played that day, all the scores. So there are advantages. But I'd sooner go back to manual, to the pen.'

BYRON'S BRIEF DOESN'T stop at dots and ticks. He drove the kit van in 1993, baggage man personified, but had his first heart attack just a month after the Sunday League was won at Canterbury, and has foregone the privilege since. At home games, meanwhile, he mans the PA. They call him 'Dasher' after Peter 'Dasher' Denning, the straw-haired Somerset favourite of the Seventies, and it is in that latter guise that his extrovert nature bubbles to the fore. The chirp of the natural raconteur remains firmly intact. Not for nothing did Geoff Blackburn, the Leicestershire scorer, label him 'the comedian of the circuit'. The badge is worn with distinct pride. And a self-deprecating titter. 'Perhaps I just know more jokes than him.'

There have been slip-ups – how could there not? Much mirth ensues whenever he announces Dean Cosker as 'Darren Cosker' and Darren Thomas as 'Dean Thomas', as is his wont. Waqar Younis was doubtless less tickled to be rechristened 'Waqar Hussain'. Writing in *The Scorer*, the aforementioned Dr Andrew Hignell, teacher, historian, scorer for BBC Radio Wales, Hon. Statistician for Glamorgan CCC and all-round gent, recalled some of Dasher's less flustered flourishes. Like that tea-time at postage-stamp Abergavenny when Worcestershire had run up 500 and he prefaced his recitation of the home bowling figures with a public health warning: 'Please could parents with young children cover the ears of their offspring.' And that day at Pontypridd when Hampshire romped home early courtesy of a spiteful spell from Malcolm

Marshall, prompting the deadpan suggestion that any spectators feeling entitled to a refund 'should write to M.D. Marshall c/o Hampshire CCC'. Or when 'Lord Byron of Beaufort' (his alternative nickname) welcomed visiting officials and followers by conveying his heartfelt thanks for their contribution to the cost of the Severn Bridge.

Not that there are no drawbacks to riding two horses with one behind. 'We use a walkie-talkie to contact the scorebox but that can be tricky if you've got a microphone in your hand as well. You can pick up the wrong thing. One day Mervyn Kitchen was umpiring at this end and he turns to signal a wide. At that very moment Alan Jones, the scoreboard operator, picked up his walkie-talkie to me and asked, "Was that a wide?" I said "yes", only I hadn't picked up the walkie-talkie. It looked as if I was agreeing with Merv's decision, granting my royal approval. Merv turned round, hands on hips, gave me a real glare.'

Byron's best friend on the circuit was Surrey's Tom Billson. 'We loved similar things. Good music, good books, shared interests. Music in particular. We used to drive them mad in the committee room at The Oval: we used to sing – and they could hear us because we used to sit quite close by. We'd check the bowling figures in plainsong. Great fun. One time when Glamorgan were sinking to defeat on the last afternoon I asked Tom if he'd join me in *Abide With Me*. We were soul mates. When he died … 1989 was it?'

'Yes,' concurs Olwen, sighing.

'Well, when he died a lot of fun went out of it as far as I was concerned. I enjoy being with all the scorers, particularly Len Chandler at Sussex, but it's not quite the same. I'm a collector and sender of postcards, probably in the thousands by now. Len and I exchange cards now, just as Tom and I did. And now Tom's wife Ruby sends me one a week.'

A COUPLE OF Sophia Gardens regulars walk by schlepping carrier bags and Sunday papers. They spot Byron and Olwen. 'No homes to go to have you?' joshes one.

'No, no home at all,' laughs Byron. 'Never leave the place. We don't want to leave the shed, you see.'

'Have you seen the size of the space they've got behind the scoreboard?' exclaims the taller passer-by. 'There's more than a scoreboard going in there.'

'I really don't know what the design is,' replies Byron. 'I think more of the present than the future,' he adds, turning to me.

'Winter well, all,' chirps the shorter passer-by. 'And you,' chorus the Dennings in perfect harmony.

So, let's go back to this time last year, to Taunton. Husband and wife exchange wistful sighs. 'Wonderful day,' exults Olwen. 'Very emotional,' affirms

Byron. 'We all felt a bit dazed. It was like when we beat Kent at Canterbury to win the Sunday League. You expected to be exhilarated but there was this quiet disbelief almost. Something had been achieved that you never dreamt you'd do. I've always been a pessimist, so it's difficult to realise that I'm now the most successful scorer Glamorgan have ever had. *Two* trophies. I still can't believe it.

'The funny thing was, I'd always thought of myself as a jinx. I joined the Glamorgan committee in 1970, the year after we last won the title, and we didn't do anything again until 1993. Cross Keys won the unofficial Welsh rugby championship in 1935–36; I first watched them in 1936–37: they've not won anything since. My son was very keen on Newport County FC, so I decided to take out a season ticket the year after they won the Welsh Cup. We saw them give Carl Zeiss Jena a shock in the European Cup-Winners' Cup but they soon went out of existence. Now it's all been ruined.

'At the end Olwen and a friend came into the box at Taunton, put their arms around me. I couldn't talk. I was deeply overcome. I remember going over to the dressing-room. Everyone was hugging everybody and I wanted to cry. So I didn't speak. If I had I would have cried.'

Did he join the team in their post-match roistering? 'No. It wasn't that I didn't think I *should* celebrate with them, it was knowing *how* they would celebrate. A bit much for an old man. I'm no teetotaller – and we certainly wet our grandchild's head last night, didn't we …?'

Olwen grins.

'… but I certainly couldn't keep up with *them*. No, we went out with friends to a local cafe.'

Olwen shakes her head slowly, the correction gentle. 'No we didn't, we had a meal at the hotel, don't you remember?'

'No, I'm talking about the championship, last year.'

Olwen smiles, a sweet, indulgent sort of smile. 'I know. We sat around the bar at the hotel then had a meal there.'

'Well, there you are,' smirks Byron. 'Ah, I remember it well …'

In league with the Gods (and others)… A Caribbean quintet of Lancashire League *alumni* during Geoffrey Gowland's prime. Clockwise from top left: Gary Sobers, prince of all-rounders, with Conrad Hunte, opener supreme and tireless worker for UNESCO (*Allsport/Hulton Getty*); Roy Gilchrist, ferocious fast bowler and confirmed maverick, pictured after a 1960 car crash (*Hulton Getty*); Sonny Ramadhin, whose cunningly-disguised leg-breaks – some of which, he confessed half a century later, he threw – brought West Indies their first Test victory in England, 1950 (*Allsport/Hulton Deutsch*); Frank Worrell, the West Indies' first regular black captain, prepares for duty at Fenners, 1950 (*Hulton Getty*)

(*All photographs this spread Graham Goldwater*)

Left: The gang's all here... Geoffrey Gowland, Steve Thorpe and Willie Hartley, Rochdale Cricket Club, October 1998

Right: John Bloody Reid... Geoffrey tells the author how he cut the captain of New Zealand down to size

Left: Over the fence... Willie Hartley demonstrates how far he drove that ball from Sobers

Bottom: Geoffrey in full flow, recounting the day he tamed Gilchrist

Gilly con carne... Geoffrey makes short work of Roy Gilchrist (*Geoffrey Gowland Collection*)

Frankly majestic... (left) Frank Worrell sweeps against England at Trent Bridge, 1957 and (right) turns his arm over against Surrey at The Oval, 1950 (*Allsport/Hulton Deutsch*)

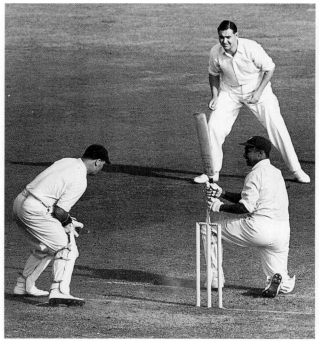

Chapter 10:
The Stalwart's Tale

'At the end of that first game [for Enfield] Bobby Marshall introduced me to Auntie Bertha and her husband, Uncle Walt. They kept a fish and chip shop in Clayton-le-Moors, Accrington, just a hundred yards from the Enfield Cricket Club. They instantly took me under their care and offered to look after my laundry for me. Auntie Bertha laundered my cricket shirts, vests, socks and hankies, and sent my trousers and sweaters to the nearby laundry. This saved me from having to lug my kit three times a week by bus from Chorley.'

Conrad Hunte, Enfield, Barbados and West Indies

IN Woody Allen's Broadway Danny Rose, *a covey of comedians convene round a table at the Carnegie Deli in Manhattan for an afternoon of cud-chewing. The yarns and punchlines fly slick and fast, each sports-jacketed Catskills veteran striving desperately to trump his predecessor with the definitive opus on Danny Rose, a fondly-regarded if comically ineffectual theatrical agent. Granted, the Bird in t'Hand pub in Rochdale may be rather a far cry from a Jewish delicatessen on 57th and Broadway, yet to be a fly on those musty walls on a Monday lunchtime in October was to experience much the same amiably competitive frisson.*

For comics read cricketers. For Danny Rose read Cec Pepper, Roy Gilchrist and Sir Gary Sobers. My guests were three alumni from the Central Lancashire League, one of the few stages on Earth that still regularly permits unpaid zealots to stand shoulder-to-shoulder and toe-to-toe with hard-boiled professionals. Sport as escape and reality. Sport as the last great leveller, the ultimate unifier.

In ascending order of ripeness: Steve Thorpe, forty-something seamer, *Daily Telegraph* cricket reporter and Caribbean adventurer, a once-stout servant of Rochdale CC, champions for five of the past eight seasons; Wilson 'Willie' Hartley, now retired from the gas board, a Rochdale mainstay from 1950 to 1978, the only living person in the CLL's lengthy and illustrious history to aggregate 5000 runs and 500 wickets for the same club, and almost certainly the only amateur bowler on the planet boasting a swagbag containing five Test captains (Sobers, Boycott, Brearley, Rohan Kanhai and Fazal Mahmood); and Geoffrey 'GV' Gowland, a former sparring partner and colleague of Steve's father, Roland. A man born to play to the gallery.

A sometime rugby league winger for Rochdale Hornets and Swinton before setting up a company selling tills and weighing machines, GV's flamboyant batting and fearlessly acidic tongue antagonised opponents of Castelton Moor CC and Rochdale for nigh-on half a century. No other non-pro has matched his feat of registering at least one fifty at every CLL venue. One of his Broadway counterparts notes that the Carnegie menu proffers a sandwich known as the Danny Rose (chopped liver or salt beef, I can never remember); were the Bird in t'Hand ever to erect such a culinary statue to GV, the filling would be rare roast beef with lashings of Colman's.

FORMED IN 1892, two years after the more celebrated Lancashire League, the CLL was once a prolific nursery. Frank Tyson and Brian Statham were among the jewels unearthed here, so too Geoff 'Noddy' Pullar, Jackie Bond and John Abrahams, and, of more recent vintage, Chris Schofield, England's great white leg-spin hope. League officials like nothing better than to point out that that grand slow left-armer Hedley Verity initially came to Yorkshire's attention when he was acting as pro for Middleton. Above them all towered Sydney Francis Barnes, by common consent the finest of all English bowlers, who preferred to ply his wares for Rochdale and Castleton Moor than Lancashire, mostly because the wage packet was fatter. These days the CLL exerts no such influence; contact between league and county club is next to non-existent. Not that there is any less antipathy between the leagues themselves. Which goes some way to explaining the cussedness that persuaded these proud institutions alone to make strenuous objections in the autumn of 1997 when the England and Wales Cricket Board's Raising The Standard masterplan advocated a nationwide network of premier leagues.

Long before the first-class counties began their import drive in 1968, the Lancastrian leagues played host to a veritable Commonwealth of talent, men for whom a blustery summer in northern England constituted the sole means of earning a crust in flannels outside their own domestic seasons. The Caribbean influx was especially strong; Sobers, Lord Learie Constantine and Sir Frank Worrell, to cite merely the most fêted, all strutted their magnificent stuff. Overseas notables are still drawn, albeit primarily from the lower echelons: in 1998 Pakistan's Asif Mujtaba was resident at Norden, the West Indies' Hamesh Anthony at Littleborough, Sri Lanka's Champaka Ramanayeke at Unsworth. Nor will it have gone unnoticed in Yorkshire that the editor of *Wisden* still prefers to donate two of his precious pages to the Red Rose leagues while those in God's own purported county get lumped in with all the riff-raff.

Things, all the same, are assuredly not what they were. Time was when 5000 folk would flock to Rochdale or Castleton Moor on a Saturday for an afternoon of boundless beer and boundaries, but as pub hours expanded, audiences inevitably dwindled. Castelton Moor ceased operations nearly two decades ago, prompting GV to see out his career at Rochdale. Not that the latter, their Dane Street ground promised 'to the people of Rochdale in perpetuity', had averted heartache. Having barely escaped the noose in 1975, a squash section fuelled a revival until the early Eighties, when the club began haemorrhaging members anew. Asda, the supermarket behemoth, purchased the premises for £2.25 million. 'Once we'd paid the debts there was nothing left,' laments Willie. The neatly-ordered red-brick pavilion testifies to the new order. The profits come from wedding receptions.

Summer's end finds GV in reflective mood. Our rendezvous had been delayed: Dot, his wife, had been gravely ill. Three weeks ago they'd switched off her life-support system. It had not been a ruffle-free marriage but the sense of loss was palpable. I would fully understand, I assured him, if he decided this was no time for fripperies; he insisted we went ahead. What better distraction, after all, than a frippery?

DRAMATIS PERSONAE:
GV: Geoffrey Gowland
Willie: Wilson Hartley
Steve: Steve Thorpe

How did you meet GV, Willie?

 Willie: We played against each other.
 GV: I used to sing and he used to put the records on [*cue first of innumerable chortles*].

You've each pitted your wits against a few vaunted professionals in your time, but many of them were past their best by then: did they always pull their fingers out?

 Willie: Most gave everything because they had to have a job the next year. In 1949, the year before I joined, Rochdale signed Charlie Barnett, the old Gloucestershire and England opener, as a pro, and in his first season he scored 1000-odd runs and took 40 wickets. Very honest, dedicated pro but of course he hadn't done well enough. At the age of forty, by the way. He went to Alf Gover's school in the winter to learn how to bowl, with Alf. The following season he scored 1000 runs and took 100 wickets. Remarkable dedication.
 GV: Talking about Alf Gover, we had another great fast bowler at The Moor, similar in style to Alf, W.H. Andrews, Bill Andrews, the 'Hand That Bowled Bradman' and all that. He was our pro when I first made the first team at sixteen. The first time I saw him his legs were covered in bandages. All he'd had to do after the war was one more season for Somerset and he'd have been entitled to a benefit, but they didn't even have the decency to give him that, so he came to us. One day he gave me a lift to the station and just as I was getting out he said, 'son, you can play the game'.
 I'd played my first game at thirteen. My elder brother Stanley was in the first team and he used to bring me along to score. Got to Oldham one day and we were a man short – and the rules stipulated that if you didn't have a full side by twenty to three you conceded the match, so I was drafted in. Their pro – I'll call him P – bowled me a long hop and I edged it for four. 'What a pissin' shot that was,' he said. So I replied, 'And what a pissin' ball that was'.
 Willie: It was Cecil George Pepper [*legendary uncompromising Australian*].

Steve, GV: Aaah …

GV: Nah, it was before Pepper.

Willie: There are lots of Cec Pepper stories.

Steve: I know. I've got a book full of 'em waiting to be published.

Willie: I'll tell you my favourite Cec Pepper story. He's playing in the Lancashire League, for Burnley, and there was an ex-sergeant-major standing as umpire, name of Tom Long. Won't stand for any bad behaviour. Anyway, Cec has his usual two or three shouts for lbw, plumb in front – not out, not out, not out. So Cec lets fly at this ump, four-letter words, the lot, so the Burnley skipper comes over and says, ''Ere, I think you've overstepped the mark, Cec. You'll be fined and not likely to play for the next six weeks.' 'All right,' says Cec, 'I'll apologise.' So he does. 'That's all right,' says Tom, 'as long as we understand each other. I like a man who speaks his mind.' So next over Cec appeals for lbw again and Tom says, 'Not out, you fat Australian bastard.'

GV: *I'll* tell you a Cec Pepper story. After the war, because of the Lord's Day Observance Society, we weren't supposed to play games on a Sunday, but there was one ground where the police used to shut their eyes, a little ground at Thornham between Rochdale and Middleton. We used to play these celebrity matches, So-and-so's XI *v* So-and-so's XI – we couldn't use the name of the club. Cec used to organise them, bringing in Australian servicemen who'd been released before our lads were. You couldn't charge for admission so you were asked to give a donation when you bought a programme. At the end of the game the sponsor asked one of these Aussies whether he'd got the £30 he'd left in his shoe – they always used to do that. This bloke was well pissed off. 'I only got twenty,' he said. Turned out Cec, who was responsible for distributing the fees, had put twenty quid in all their shoes and pocketed £10 for himself each time.

Steve: Tell some Gilly stories.

GV: We had the pleasure of a West Indian gentleman called Roy Gilchrist, who'd been sent home from a tour of India in 1959, so Oldham signed him.

Willie: Middleton.

GV: No, no.

Willie: He never played for Oldham. He played for Crompton and Middleton.

GV: I'll bow down to your greater knowledge. Anyway, this Gilchrist was sent home from India, for bowling beamers and other misdemeanours, and everybody in the league objected to him as well. No-ball, no-ball, no-ball, the umpires kept calling. But what could the league do? He'd already got the money in his back pocket, before he'd even started.

Willie: Ooh, he was a bugger. Mind you, I don't think he quite got all of it.

GV: Anyway, this Gilchrist has the audacity to bowl two or three beamers, at *my* head. First one, four pennyworth, thanks very much; next one four pennyworth, thank you very much. So he started bowling yorkers and I hit him all over the bloody field, so he came down the pitch and said, 'What are you doing to me?' In future, I said, keep 'em there. Taught me how to hook, that did.

Willie: What about George Holland? Before going out to face Gilly he took fifty minutes to pad up! Foam rubber on chest, towels on thighs, shin pads on arms. Gilly's first ball knocked seven of his teeth out; mind you, the newspaper said they were false. 'Is he quick?' wondered the next man in as they crossed. 'What do you think?' said George, spitting his teeth out.

Steve: That reminds me of a story my dad told me of when he was batting with you, GV, at The Moor. You were one for four, dire straits. Gilly pushes off from the sightscreen, and as he gets to the end of his run you put your hand up. You batted in glasses, didn't you?

GV: Yes, I had to.

Steve: You stopped him and said, 'Excuse me Roy, just a little spot of rain on the glass.' He was fuming.

GV: I was quite entitled.

Steve: Apparently, Gilly turned round to my dad and said, 'This man very very big-headed man'. 'Yeah,' said my dad, 'he is a bit', not wishing to ruffle his feathers further.

GV: Your dad was scared to get up the other end. He was, though, the only man to ever hit him for six. Off a tennis shot it was.

Willie: Another Gilly story. Jean and I were on holiday in Scotland, eating in the hotel restaurant. Fella behind the bar had an MCC tie on. Can't recall his name but he'd been captain of Hertfordshire, member of the MCC committee and managing director of Beecham's in the north, the pharmaceutical company. Every year he used to take a team to play a company team representing the southern division and one year he asked Gilly to play for him. Denis Compton was playing for the opposition, and at one point Gilly bowled him a beamer. Compton really lost it, started swearing. In a friendly match!

GV: May I just finish *my* Gilly story? In the Oldham Green 'Un one night they had a headline, 'Gilchrist Brands Wife With Flat Iron'. He'd come back from driving his wagon – he also had a delivery job – and his trousers weren't pressed. Never liked to bowl at 130 miles an hour without pleats in his flannels. So he grabbed the iron and said, 'I'll iron them meself' and it inadvertently touched his wife's skin. Went to court. Not long after he turned up at a match and some-body said, 'You're the effer who branded his wife with a flat iron'. Gilly went beresk. Took his knife out and stabbed this bloke. Got six months.

Steve: I interviewed Gilly a few years ago in a pub in Oldham and I asked him about that. 'Stephen,' he said, 'the iron was not hot.' I still see him in Jamiaca – a sad, frail figure drinking lots of white rum.

How well did these blokes get paid?

Willie: Very well. Gilly would have been on £2000 a summer, perhaps £1500. Charles Barnett was on £1200. Then there were the collections if you did well. And remember we used to get crowds of 4000 to 5000. Those were the days of the five-and-a-half-day week, and very few cars, so people would come down to the club as soon as they finished work on a Saturday. At one match in 1950, when I was thirteen and only the twelfth man, I think there were *five* collections. My share came to £3.50. My father, who drove a horse and cart, earned £2.50 a *week*.

GV: And do bear in mind that pubs shut at 2 p.m. but the cricket clubs stayed open all afternoon, so the crowds came. They put loads of money in my collections they were so drunk.

Willie: We'd get all the non-member boozers. The crowds were really quite belligerent.

GV: Another Cec Pepper story. We were playing Radcliffe on Whit Monday, Cec's club. I opened with Vijay Manjrekar [*Indian Test player Denis Compton ran out with a left-footed volley at Alf Gover's behest – Ed*] and this murmur started going round the crowd, a titter. It was a beautiful track, Manjrekar's on 46 and I'm struggling on 40, half off the edge. Cec asks me what the murmur's about. I explained that Manjrekar only wanted four to be the quickest ever to 1000 in a Central Lancashire League season. 'I'll tell you what I'll do,' said Cec, I'll give him one.' So Cec bowls him a googly, bounces one, two, three times and bowls him.

Steve: He was crying afterwards, so my dad tells me.

GV: Yes, yes – and he blamed it all on me. I just lay on the ground as he walked off and pissed meself laughing.

Steve: Manjrekar was frightened to death of Cec. Cec used to come up to him in the bar and call him all sorts of names. My dad told the story of the day Cec went up to him at the end of play and sees him in one of his stripey blazers – bit like you, GV. You're looking very sober today. Anyway, Cec goes up to Manjrekar says, 'Which horse d'you pull that fookin' thing from?' Vijay, a shy man, was mortified.

Willie: I remember my first game against Cec as a youngster. Hadn't got a clue about reading googlies or flippers. Michael Fleming, a very respected senior cricketer, was batting at the other end when I came in and he came down the wicket. 'All you've got to do,' he said, 'is play forward and if he pitches one up and it's a half-volley hit it back over his head. If you do that he'll come up to you and say, "right, son, you can open your eyes now".' So Cec pitches one up, I hit it back over his head for six and he did just what Michael predicted. So when he's finished saying, 'You can open your effin eyes now', I said, 'I won't need to if you bowl any more crap like that.' If you answered him back he loved you. We were quite good friends after that.

GV: We used to have some really top-class professionals, and they were invariably the club captains. We had Vinoo Mankad, Rochdale had Phadkar, John Reid was at Heywood.

Steve: Tell them that story you told me earlier about John Reid.

GV: Ooh aye. We were playing at Heywood and this John Reid, I admired him. At half past one, an hour before the start, he'd be out there with his team for fielding practice. We'd never seen *that* before. Reid was in great form, too. I was only eighteen, working selling bacon slicers. Always went for a drink on a Saturday morning when I picked my wages up from Mr Manchester. I told him I was going to play against John Reid that afternoon, so I should only have a couple of halves of Bass. You want to have one of those vitamin tablets, he said. So I went to the chemist and bought some then distributed them among some of my team-mates. When I batted I was going nineteen to the dozen. Bang, bang, bang. Hardly put a foot wrong. Then John bowls me one outside off. Right, I thought, this one's going. So I smack it back but this bugger dives, just gets his fingertips under it but not before it had bounced about a foot in front of him. But he still says, 'Zat'. Well, thought the umpire, he's captain of New Zealand, he must be right. So he gave me out. Boy did the crowd boo. So Reid comes into the pavilion afterwards and says, 'I've never cheated anyone out in my life'. I'm not sure, when I was in the gully and Mr Reid had only eleven on the board, whether the ball touched my toes or boot before I caught it, but it sure was compensation. Reid turned round to me and said it hit the ground. So I said, 'Eff off to New Zealand'. Happy days.

It must have been a very satisfying way of cutting these guys down to size …

Willie: Oh yes. Remember Sid Barnes, opened for Australia with Arthur Morris after the war? Came to Rochdale one day to play in a benefit match for Charles Barnett. We had a real character in those days called Frank Schofield, The Bomber.

GV: Fast bowler, cracker.

Willie: Anyway, Sid comes in and Bomber positions himself at short leg, just in front of the bat. Barnes went mad. After a few balls he pops one up, Bomber sticks an arm up and takes this great catch, pure reflex. 'They haven't come to watch you field,' snapped Barnes, 'they've come to watch me bat.' 'Well,' said Bomber, 'they won't see so fookin' much of you today.'

How did your wives and loved ones feel about you spending so much time away from them?

GV: My late wife liked nothing better than when I had a good collection. She'd go through my trousers, take the money out of the back pocket and go out and spend it.

Steve: She was more famous than you, GV. I remember her as a kid, whooping it up, dancing on the tables. You did that too when you scored a fifty, mind. What about that time Dot set fire to all your cricket gear? And threw it out the window.

GV: That's an exaggeration.

Steve: Oh, you told me that several years ago.

GV: She wouldn't have got anywhere near the window. She'd have got the old hand-off.

Steve: You'd gone away with some girl, don't you remember it?

GV: I'd just taken some money to the bank.

Given such a cosmopolitan league, was there much racism?

Willie: No, not that I can remember. The only bloke I didn't get on with was Ralph Legall, the West Indies wicketkeeper. Played with Rochdale as an amateur at the end of his career. Always world-weary, slumping about. Didn't want to keep but his bowling was no great shakes, so our captain, John McMahon, a tough Australian, said he might as well keep. An Indian lad fielding at short third man missed a catch and John, who was a bit of a racist, started having a right go, calling him all the obvious names. So Ralph flings his gloves off, runs over to John and says, 'Don't call my fellow a so-and-so'. It took five or six of us to calm him down.

Steve: Dad told me about the time Manjrekar arrived at Castleton Moor. Had a couple of net sessions and hundreds, literally, turned up to watch. Then the team was posted up on the board for the first game of the season and his name wasn't even on it! Somebody forgot! Cliff Parker, the chairman of selectors.

GV: Best defensive batsman I ever saw.

Willie: Wouldn't entertain you, stay all afternoon for fifty. And not give you a ball to face. Castleton Moor once played Werneth when Tommy Greenhough [*last England leg-spinner to take five wickets in a Test innings – Ed*] was deputy pro there: Manjrekar would shout 'googly ball' before he'd bowled it. He'd spot it from the hand.

Steve: Tommy apparently packed it in after a couple of overs.

GV: He used to do that with Sonny Ramadhin. No one else had a clue. Read him from the pitch.

Willie: One season in the late Forties, early Fifties, Crompton had a very poor side and only reached one hundred three times; they still won the league! Ramadhin bowled every side out for under 100! Magic bowler. I was standing in as wicketkeeper once a few years later and I said to him, 'You can't expect me to pick you, Sonny'. 'Don't worry,' he said, 'all I bowl now is two balls – the leg-break and the off-break, and I bowl the leg-break from higher.' What he didn't tell me was that it was only about half an inch higher.

Steve: I opened the bowling with him in that match. A great honour.

Is Sonny still around?

Steve: Yeah, yeah. Used to have a pub in Delph, but the brewery took it over after twenty-five years and left poor Sonny in limbo.

GV: The White Lion. We called in there on the way back from rugby once. Someone said it didn't open until seven. 'They'll open for me,' I said. So I banged on the bloody door, threw one or two pebbles at the window. His wife opens the window and tells us to go away. Then Sonny comes down and says to come round the front. But they kept putting the rent up. Didn't even have the decency to offer him another pub. What about one near Old Trafford? Imagine, Sonny Ramadhin running a pub near Old Trafford!

Steve: Broke his heart. He's got diabetes as well of course, and cataracts are limiting his golf now too. His grandson plays for Lancashire schoolboys.

Why did the Lancashire leagues attract so many more distinguished players than those in Yorkshire?

GV: More money.

Hence Sir Gary signing for Radcliffe ...

Willie: Best player the leagues ever had, no argument.

GV: Hear, hear. But what about another great man who played at Radcliffe before Sir Garfield – Sir Frank Worrell? I batted against him. Fast bowler then, and a fantastic batsman. The way he would just step back and thread a shot between square leg and mid-on. I couldn't do that. I tried.

Willie: Sobers had three shots for every ball. Mind you, the highlight of my career was bowling him. Knocked his middle stump out. In fairness, though, I have to say the ball was a bit short. He lifted his bat up and was going to murder the thing but the ball shot and he didn't get it down quick enough. Nice man.

Steve: Hammered me all over the field once, d'you remember? When he was at Littleborough, '75. I'd had a week in Anglesey with my girlfriend and came back absolutely knackered, just for this game. One for 43 off four overs after Sir Gary came in at number five. I bowled like a drain.

Willie: I played against Radcliffe when he was there, an evening match. Radcliffe won the toss and batted. Sobers came in at number three. Radcliffe lost a wicket in the first over and Sobers came in at 25 to seven. At quarter to seven he was 50; after three more overs he'd made 100. Before seven o'clock! Never seen anything like that in me life.

GV: Don't mention it. That time he hammered you, Steve, I had a big appeal for a catch against him turned down: went on to make eighty. He was knighted that same year. It was there on the scorecard: Sir Gary Sobers. Talking about dodgy decisions, I played against Werneth once on this ground which had a slope and their pro was Fazal Mahmood [*former Pakistan captain and architect of his country's first Test win against England at The Oval in 1954 – Ed*]. What a great bowler he was. I'm batting and he's bowling leg-cutters, which as a left-hander are off-cutters to me. Gets one to go away from me down the slope and appeals – 'How-zzzattt'. So the umpire sticks his finger up. Afterwards I went up to him in the bar and said, 'Excuse me, Mr Mahmood: off-cutter to me, pitching on leg-stump, going down the slope – and you appeal?' So he touches me on the shoulder and says, 'Sorry son, it's me living'.

Did umpires give the pros the benefit of the doubt?

GV: Oh yes, I think so.

Willie: The odd one. Most of them were pretty honest and honourable people.

Steve: I had Ambrose plumb lbw the first ball Curtly ever faced in the league, on his debut for Heywood. Umpire looked the other way, but I bowled him next ball to make sure. Bit of a mistake, that. He roared in later and shattered us with eight for forty-five, me included.

GV: But people came to see runs scored and the most likely to do that were the pros.

Steve: The amateur strength was very good then, not like it is now.

Willie: There are still a lot of good players but the supporting players aren't what they used to be. One reason there aren't so many good bowlers is because we're playing overs cricket. We used to have to bowl a side out to win.

Not if you bowled first. Were you obliged to declare at tea?

GV: No, but it was understood. If you got anything like a good score you'd declare. But if you didn't the captain would be ostracised. I remember one night match against Heywood. We used to play night games on Tuesdays and Wednesdays, six-thirty to nine each night. Haywood got about 180, 190, not enough to declare, then batted on 'til quarter past seven the next night. It was a hot night, I can see it now, and this Australian, Ray Hogan, white shirt black with sweat, really has a go at their captain. When we batted their captain got nought for 132, Hogan goes mad and we'd won the bloody match at five to eight!

Willie: Come on.

GV: All right, five to nine.

AND ON THEY went, paying homage and blowing raspberries, teasing and tittering. Inches conjured into feet, memories into myths, embers into flames. Handing on the torch.

Bibliography

Arlott, John *Fred: Portrait of a Fast Bowler* (Methuen, 1971)

Bose, Mihir *Sporting Colours – Sport and Politics in South Africa* (Robson Books, 1994)

Botham, Ian with Hayter, Peter *Botham: My Autobiography (Don't Tell Kath)* (HarperCollins, 1994)

Boycott, Geoff with Brindle, Terry *Boycott: The Autobiography* (Macmillan, 1987)

Close, Brian with Mosey, Don *I Don't Bruise Easily* (Macdonald and Janes, 1978)

Cowdrey, Colin *MCC: The Autobiography of a Cricketer* (Coronet, 1976)

D'Oliveira, Basil with Murphy, Patrick *Time To Declare* (J.M. Dent & Sons, 1980)

Foot, David *From Grace to Botham* (Redcliffe Press, 1980)

—— *Harold Gimblett: Tormented Genius of Cricket* (Star, 1984)

—— *Cricket's Unholy Trinity* (Stanley Paul, 1985)

—— *Sunshine Sixes and Cider: A History of Somerset CC* (David & Charles, 1986)

—— *Country Reporter* (David & Charles, 1992)

—— *Beyond Bat and Ball* (Good Books, 1993)

—— *Wally Hammond: The Reasons Why* (Robson Books, 1996)

Foot, David with Richards, Viv *Viv Richards* (World's Work, 1979)

Foot, David with Abbas, Zaheer *Zed* (World's Work, 1983)

Gover, Alfred *The Long Run* (Pelham, 1991)

Hampshire, John with Mosey, Don *Family Argument – My 20 Years in Yorkshire Cricket* (Allen & Unwin, 1983)

Hill, Alan *Peter May: A Biography* (Andre Deutsch, 1996)

Lloyd, Grahame *Daffodil Days* (Gomer, 1998)

Lock, Tony *For Surrey and England* (Hodder & Stoughton, 1957)

Procter, Mike with Murphy, Patrick *South Africa: The Years of Isolation and the Return to International Cricket* (Lennard Queen Anne Press, 1994)

Root, Fred *A Cricket Pro's Lot* (Arnold, 1937)

Ross, Alan *Australia '63* (The Pavilion Library, 1991)

Sheppard, David *Parson's Pitch* (Hodder & Stoughton, 1964)

West, Peter *Clean Sweep* (W.H. Allen, 1987)

West, Peter *Flannelled Fool and Muddied Oaf* (Star, 1987)

Whittington, R.S. *Simpson's Safari* (Heinemann, 1967)

Williams, Charles *Bradman* (Little Brown, 1996)

Plus various newspapers and *Wisden Cricketers Almanack*, *Playfair Cricket Annual*, *Wisden Cricket Monthly* and *The Cricketer*.

Acknowledgements

WHERE does a boy start? Thanks above all, to Alf, David, Brian, Don, Peter, David, Ali, John, Byron and Geoffrey, for their time, their patience, their indulgence and their constructive criticism. It was a pleasure and a privilege making your acquaintance, gentlemen. Ditto Wilson Hartley, who has my undying gratitude for getting Geoffrey to the pub on time. To Olwen Denning, Frank Keating, Mike Roseberry, Lady Sheppard and Mike Smith, for adding their ha'p'orths. To Eddie Bevan, Andrew Hignell, Norman de Mesquita (get well soon), Martin Searby and especially Steve Thorpe, for nudges and path-smoothing. To David Summerfield for literary supplies at short notice. To Huw Richards for his customary promptings. To Jeremy Novick (he knows why). To Frank Keating (again) and Matthew Engel (they know why). To Virgin Trains/Great Western Railways for ferrying me about with acceptable punctuality. To John Pawsey, my angelic agent (now there's two words you don't often see occupying the same sentence!) To all at David & Charles, in particular my infinitessimally patient editor Sue Viccars – for passing the ball and letting me run with it. To Graham 'Hoy Hoy' Goldwater – lecturer, carpenter, proprietor of Glass Onion Inc, guitarist to the gentry and snapper of superfine snaps. Thanks for letting him out, Carol. And, of course, to Anne, Laura, Josef, Woody and Evie, the last-named cooked just in time to see her daddy give birth in rather less arduous circumstances than her mummy.

Index